Living
in a Glass
House

Living *in a* Glass House

Surviving the Scrutiny of Ministry and Marriage

DONALD HARVEY
GENE WILLIAMS

Beacon Hill Press of Kansas City
Kansas City, Missouri

Copyright 2002
by Beacon Hill Press of Kansas City

ISBN 083-411-9544

Printed in the
United States of America

Cover Design: Michael Walsh

10 9 8 7 6 5 4 3 2 1

Contents

103631

About the Authors

Donald Harvey holds a master of arts degree in counseling and a doctorate in marriage and family therapy. Having been a marital therapist for more than 25 years, he has counseled numerous clergy couples. He previously served as the clinical director of a Christian counseling agency and supervised a national crisis line specifically for parsonage families. Donald has extensive experience with radio and television interviews and has written several books and magazine articles on marriage. He and his wife of more than 28 years, Jan, conduct marriage enrichment retreats and seminars and provide intensive therapy experiences for clergy marriages in crisis.

Gene Williams earned a bachelor of arts degree from Trevecca Nazarene University and a master of divinity degree from Nazarene Theological Seminary. After nearly 50 years of successful pastoral ministry, Gene founded and directs Shepherds' Fold, a support ministry to clergy and their families. He was married to Bettye for 30 years until her death from cancer. His wife of 8 years, Joyce, joins him in implementing the activities of Shepherds' Fold. As an affiliate with the Billy Graham Evangelistic Association, Gene travels extensively and is a frequent speaker at ministry conferences and retreats for pastors and their spouses.

Foreword

Donald Harvey and Gene Williams come from two different backgrounds—one is a pastor and one is a counselor. But they share a single passion—to rescue or enhance the marriages of ministry couples. As you read what they have to say about ministry marriages, you will say to yourself, "I knew that! Why didn't I ever think to do that?" Their message is simply profound—and profoundly simple.

The authors don't offer you a quick fix. For long-established bad habits there are no instant or easy cures. Harvey and Williams point you in the right direction and encourage each step, but it will be your own heart commitment that keeps you going forward.

You can scan this book and see a friend, a coworker, and maybe your spouse in its pages. You might even be tempted to share the book with someone—perhaps even underlining a few sections that you feel pertain especially to him or her. But first, we encourage you to pore over this book, applying each page to yourself. Ask yourself, "Do I need to implement this in my life?" And if the shoe fits, put it on and wear it.

—**Dr. Robert Coleman**

More than 50 years ago, God called us into full-time Christian service. Secretly, I hoped my job would be that of a minister's wife. My Mr. Perfect had come along, and we set out in ministry. We were young and full of enthusiasm to reach the world for Christ. But when a new door opened and my husband embraced the call to seminary teaching, I whimpered for a couple of years over loss of ministry. Eventually God opened my eyes, and I saw my "alongside of" place. We have willingly, even deliberately, chosen to live in a glass house through these years, and we have been blessed by it. I admit there have been times when we asked the Lord to "pull the drapes and give us time to recoup." He has been faithful and loving and good.

If you're in a ministry marriage, you'll profit from reading *Living in a Glass House*. When folks peer into *your* glass house, let them see a reflection of His glory.

—**Marietta Coleman**

Dr. and Mrs. Coleman are a former pastor and pastor's wife now minister-ing through the seminary community in the training of pastors. He serves as director of the Institute of Evangelism at the Billy Graham Center in Wheaton, Illinois, and dean of the International Schools of Evangelism for the Billy Graham Association. He is a founding member of the Lausanne Committee for World Evangelism and is currently distinguished professor of discipleship and evangelism at Gordon-Conwell Seminary in South Hamil-ton, Massachusetts.

Endorsements

- Are pastors and their spouses human? Yes!
- Can they, like other humans, make mistakes under pressure? Yes!
- Can their marriages get out of joint through the pressures of the pastorate? Yes!
- Are the skills of salvage specialists Harvey and Williams (veteran counselor, veteran pastor) sufficient, under God, to put such marriages back into shape? Yes!

For many struggling couples this book will be a lifeline. It is a privilege to commend it.

—**J. I. PACKER,** Professor of Theology, Regent College

Marriage and ministry both matter to God. He created them, and He called us to enter into them with great joy. It stands to reason, therefore, that marriage and ministry should never get in each other's way, but sadly they sometimes do. The authors are well aware of the tensions that can arise in ministry marriages, and they have brought their considerable experience to bear in this book, which will prove invaluable to all who want to be ministers whose marriages adorn their ministry.

—**JILL AND STUART BRISCOE,** Ministers at Large, Elmbrook Church

The life of a ministry couple is often complicated by stress, contentious members, and unrealized dreams. But the truth is, no one said it should or would be easy. Don and Gene paint a very positive picture of pastoral ministry and make the point that "through it all" it can be fun and very rewarding. Let's have fun along the way! It's a great read.

—**H. B. LONDON,** Vice President, Ministry Outreach/
Pastoral Ministries, Focus on the Family

With great insight and humanizing honesty, *Living in a Glass House* opens the doors to a realistic understanding of what ministry relationships are all about . . . and is a correction to the mixed motives that drive many pastors. It provides a unique perspective on priorities that enable a pastor and wife to "finish well." This book is a fresh breath!

—**DR. BILL E. BURCH,** President of Eagle Ministries, Inc.

Introduction

We're passionate about ministry, and we're passionate about marriage. *Living in a Glass House* is a book about ministry and the marriages produced by being in ministry.

It was our shared passions for ministry and marriage that brought us together on this project. Gene has spent nearly 50 years ministering to the masses and speaking to thousands on any given Sunday. He has lived his life of ministry in the trenches.

Don has spent his time counseling ministry couples one couple at a time, those usually in great conflict or pain. Despite our different perspectives, we've found that we have similar things to say to similar groups of people.

We're reminded of the time-honored poem about several blind men who were each asked to describe what he thought an elephant looked like. One touched the side of the elephant, another the trunk, another the tail, and so on. Afterward, each man described what he had felt. Their accounts and depictions were stunningly different. Each based his description of the elephant on his own limited experience.

In the same way, we come from two very different perspectives and varied experiences. We hope our "different views of the elephant" will help you see the big picture of ministry and marriage more clearly.

We have several goals for this book. First, we want it to be *real*—to accurately describe the common experiences of those in ministry. This means avoiding the temptation to paint a picture of extremes—of viewing life in the ministry as being either gloriously wonderful or the absolute pit of despair. In reality, it's neither. This need for balance is highlighted by a conversation with a friend of ours who recently returned from a pastors-and-spouses retreat. Conducted by two therapists and billed as an "uplifting getaway for ministry couples," the event was not conducted as advertised. "The retreat was so dark," he said. "They must have thought we all hated our jobs and were just miserable in the ministry."

Nothing could be farther from the truth about ministry. The rewards of ministry life are unequaled, but we admit that it's a life that has unique challenges. And these challenges affect all those in-volved—the pastor, the pastor's spouse, and their marriage.

We want this book to be *informative.* We've taken a risk and ventured into what we think a ministry marriage should look like. In essence, we're offering a definition for health—not a cookie-cutter ideal that every couple has to somehow squeeze into, but principles and benchmarks that allow you to take your own marital pulse and gain a sense of relational direction. Is your marriage heading in the right direction? Is anything interfering with your experiencing all that God has for you in your marriage? Are there things you can do to regain control of your relationship? One of our goals is to help you find answers to these questions.

We want to encourage you to step beyond facades and images and take an honest look at your marriage. Reality is what is—not what we want it to be or wish it to be, but what's actually going on. You'll see yourself and your peers in this book. From those in the trenches we hear one constant theme: Ministry marriage is unique in its challenges but not special—none of us is exempt from human frailties.

We want you to find this book *readable.* We recognize the need for a book, not a textbook. You'll find few graphs and charts here. Though we recognize that more and more women are moving into a role traditionally occupied by men, the majority of current situations tend to be more traditional. Therefore, for the sake of readability, we frequently refer to the pastor as "he" and the spouse as "she." We recognize that not all pastors and spouses fit that mold, but the principles in this book apply to all clergy marriages.

Living in a Glass House is meant to inspire hope. Through these pages we want you to see yourself and what you can become. God's design is for intimate marriages. And, believe it or not, it can happen for you—even when you're living in a glass house.

1

Gene Williams

Living in a Glass House Can Be Hazardous to Your Health

We were early for the first worship service in a small town 35 miles from home. It was my first Sunday filling the pulpit until the new pastor arrived. We weren't sure where the church building was located, so we allowed ourselves plenty of time to find it.

No one was around when we arrived, so we went next door to McDonald's to get a cup of coffee and wait for someone to open the doors. To my knowledge no one in the restaurant knew us, so I was surprised when a stranger said, "Hi, Pastor Williams. How are you?" I apologized for not recognizing him, and then he helped me out by saying, "Oh, you don't know me, but I know you. My wife and I have followed your ministry."

As they walked away, I told my wife, "I sure hope having coffee at McDonald's on Sunday is OK in this town!"

The glass house of ministry leaves no place to hide. Granted, we should live in such a way that there's nothing to hide, but we all have moments we're not proud of. The high visibility of the pastor and his family affects everyone in the household. Some ministerial homes buckle under the pressure.

Once you enter this brightly lit field of ministry, you can be sure the enemy will point out every flaw, every wart of conduct, and each miscue you make. You'll be subjected to public scrutiny under a magnifying glass, which can create great tension on the pastor and everyone around him. You can be sure that this condition can be hazardous to a marriage unless both husband and wife learn how to handle it. The stress of picture-window living can warp preachers' kids if their parents don't have a healthy approach to this lifestyle. Survival begins with the acceptance of the fact that there's no place to escape, no place to hide. Living with and accepting this awareness keeps us from potentially destructive experiences.

Getting off an airplane in Dallas, 300 miles from home, Joyce and I were waiting for our contact person when we heard a cheery, "Hi, Pastor Williams. What are you-all doing in Dallas?" It was someone who recognized us because of the visibility of our position in Wichita, Kansas. I suppose we could have seen it as an intrusion into our privacy, but it was God who gave us that visibility, and I believe this incident was a compliment from Him. He was saying, "I can trust you in the light of public scrutiny." Realizing that we're recognized because of God's call on our lives, we can choose to see these interruptions as pats on the back.

No Margin for Error

I can't count the number of times my wife and I have said to each other, "We couldn't misbehave if we wanted to!" Living with the scrutiny of ministry could make you paranoid even if you aren't doing anything wrong. You may find yourself looking over your shoulder to see who's watching, even though you aren't guilty of doing anything shameful or embarrassing. Living a public life can easily cause stress, and you may fear the pleasure of relaxation and being yourself—of simply being human. Some ministers insist upon meeting unrealistic standards of conduct, but the environment surrounding a stressed-out person is tense. Continually holding your emotions and feelings in check can cause you to become rigid, inflexible, and unreal.

May God richly bless the spouses of ministers. They're judged for what they wear and what they weigh. They're seen as uninvolved in their spouse's ministry if they simply take a backseat, or they're perceived as too pushy if they're very visible. If they take a leadership role in the congregation, they want the spotlight. If they're quiet and unassuming, they're branded as nonsupportive.

This unfair pressure may create major problems for the marriage. Many couples in ministry feel they have no life of their own and become rigid with fear. In some instances the pressure created by this scrutiny has caused good people to leave the ministry in order to save their marriages.

The First Step to Living Successfully

How do we handle the pressure of living in a glass house? Maybe it's not as difficult as it seems.

The reality is that folks have a tendency to jump to judgment. One of the first steps to living successfully in the public eye is to accept that there are no perfect people. In Matt. 7:1 Jesus said, "Do not judge, or you too will be judged." He went on to ask, "Why do you look at the speck of sawdust in your brother's eye and pay no attention to the plank in your eye?" (v. 3). Jesus was pointing out that everyone has some flaws. Be your best self, and admit that you're not perfect. Neither is your family.

I've never made a conscious decision to live that way. For me it's seemed to be a natural way of life since I've had no image to protect and no desire to hide my foibles (and I have plenty of those). I've been comfortable to just be me—and make a lot of apologies! Maybe this is our first clue to surviving in a glass house—being comfortable with being real.

Over the years it's been my privilege to speak at many pastors' conferences. At most of these I've shared a story to which many can relate—a story I felt uncomfortable acknowledging publicly. It reveals a major flaw in the parsonage family. One of my sons went through a very tough time in high school. At one point in his senior year life became unbearable for him. His friends were in a totally different social strata. Clothes, cars, and many other social differences caused him much distress. Added to that was my pressure for him to go to a Christian college rather than a state university. He broke. Just before his high school graduation, he attempted suicide. He shot himself in front of his mother and me. (This story is told in full in my book *Living in the Zoo—and Loving It!*) Fortunately, he was unsuccessful in his suicide attempt and today is a wonderful Christian husband and father.

After we've shared how God brought his mother and me through that gut-wrenching time, many ministerial parents have talked of similar experiences. A common reaction is "We've never been able to talk about it openly. We've been afraid of what people would think." They were protecting the image of pastoral family perfection. If you don't buy into the idea that you're perfect, you'll have no false facade to preserve. I always made sure I was the best person, pastor, and father I could be, and I could live with that.

Be Ye Real!

While I'm not proud about that awful incident with my son, I can't change the fact that it did indeed happen. My entire congregation knew. My son's 2,000 fellow high school students knew. He was an all-city football player and very popular with his peers. The word was out, and everyone could see through our glass walls. My son and my wife and I decided to face the incident and go on with life. As a result, we never feared someone holding that family tragedy over our heads. We chose to let the crisis in our glass house be of benefit and encouragement to others. We have received thanks from numerous pastor-parents who had been held hostage by guilt associated with a personal catastrophe that was closely scrutinized by folks peering into their glass houses.

We've always been a real family, and real families have real problems. Once you make friends with that concept, living in a glass house can be healthful, fun, and fruitful.

People Are Watching—but That's OK

Yes, we'll work at improving our weaknesses as we focus on a healthy, happy husband-wife relationship and at being good parents. We can turn our glass house into a loving, caring, crystal palace. After all, some people have never seen a warm, truly functional family. Many husbands and fathers have never had a role model. Many wives and mothers received no guidance in their families of origin as to how a Christian family functions.

People are watching us. Accept that. If we resent it, we'll experience unbearable pressure. On the other hand, since we want to be the best Christian spouses and parents we can be, why not take advantage of a great opportunity to demonstrate God's grace for daily living?

Joyce and I have come to enjoy going to restaurants, airports, and shopping areas. We never know who's going to step up and say, "I know who you are." So we look forward to meeting the people who have been peeking into our crystal palace. Learning to live as real people—out in the open—is possible and wonderful. It can provide some very interesting moments.

On a car trip from Wichita, Kansas, to Alexandria, Louisiana, we began to get hungry as we neared the Oklahoma-Texas state line. I had seen a sign advertising a seafood restaurant, and my mouth began to water, so we decided it would be worth leaving the interstate to get a great meal. We didn't realize that the restaurant was seven miles into the countryside, but since our taste buds were committed, it didn't matter. After all, it would be good to relax and enjoy ourselves in cozy seclusion. Wearing our jeans and ball caps —totally out of "uniform"—we were happy to find such a casual setting. The place was almost empty. We thought for sure we were out of our glass house.

Throughout our leisurely meal of deep-fried catfish, french fries, slaw, and hush puppies, we kept laughing about how much food we were getting on our shirts. Grease was dripping from our chins, and we teased each other about how well we were wearing our food. Finally, we pushed back from the table and headed toward the cashier to pay. I laughed as I looked down at my shirt and saw how many remnants of dinner I was wearing. I told Joyce we might want to put it in the refrigerator at our motel so that nothing would spoil.

As we stood there, a couple came up behind us, tapped us on the shoulder, and said, "It sure is good seeing you two enjoying yourselves. We watched you all during dinner from the corner over there. How have you been?" They were remote acquaintances from another church in our hometown. Hastily we made sure there was no fish grease residue on our hands as we shook theirs. I attempted to rub some ketchup from my shirt. Our smiles and responses were genuine. When we were back in the car, both of us chuckled about our lack of dignity, and I said, "So much for solitude! I'm glad we didn't eat with our fingers!"

But somehow we knew that it wouldn't have mattered. It's all right to let those on the other side of the glass see some grease on our faces. After all, we know we were in pretty good company. Jesus must have enjoyed many fish dinners. And yes, there were some people who did not approve of His social life. Remember—He ate with publicans and sinners. Shameful! He lived in a glass house but enjoyed life in spite of His critics. It was hazardous to His health, but never forget who had the last word. Our Heavenly Father spoke words of power, and the Resurrection happened. So it will be with us.

Taking a Closer Look at "Us"

What does all of this have to do with a ministerial marriage? Much more than you might think. We recognize that there are pressures in every marriage. But it's also true that marriages lived out in glass houses have exposure that others don't. With little or no margin for error, ministerial couples may feel they exist on the razor edge of impending disaster.

On the other hand, this high visibility can be used to demonstrate to those peeking through the glass walls that ministry families are just normal people. This may shock some. Many have the misperception that families involved in ministry are comprised of "supersaints." To see their pastoral family working through some of the same difficulties that they experience in their own homes is an encouragement to many church members. The key is *working through* the problems.

Living in a glass house can become an opportunity to demonstrate that God's grace is sufficient for every situation. In fact, developing a strong sense of mission and acceptance of the call to ministry can help us come to enjoy this God-given opportunity.

Even though at times your glass house may seem to shatter all around you, just remember: our Lord put you in each situation, and He has the final say. I'm sure that at times His robe may have had some grease spots too. Perhaps He even licked His fingers!

2

Donald Harvey

You're at Risk

P eter and Deb* came to me to discuss some problems they were having in their marriage. They shared how their early years together had been marked by only good times. Life just seemed to come so easily to them—at least until they decided to start a family. After several unsuccessful attempts to get pregnant, they consulted with medical specialists and spent several years trying everything suggested. Finally, after exhausting all possible options and knowing their biological clocks were ticking away, they resigned themselves to the fact that having their own biological child was never going to happen for them.

"Disappointment" understates what they felt. They were shattered, heartbroken. What they had longed for many years—something so natural and automatic for all their friends—was not going to happen for them. Using words like "unfair" and "cruel," they began to question each other and even God. "Why is this happening to us?" "Are we being punished for something we've done?" "Is it your fault?" "Is it mine?" "We have so much love to give and would be great parents—why can't we?"

Finally able to get past the blame and the grief, Peter and Deb at last arrived at a point of acceptance. They didn't like it. They didn't understand it. But they accepted it. They realized it wasn't anybody's fault—there was no one to blame. They were finally able to begin moving on with their lives. And it was with this acceptance that they first considered adoption as an alternative.

---

*Names and other identifying details have been changed in the description of this and other case histories throughout the book.

Peter and Deb reasoned that if they couldn't have a biological child, they could at least give their home and their love to a child who needed both. They soon found that adoption wasn't easy or quick. But they were resolute, and after what seemed like an eternity, their persistence was rewarded. The day they had longed for, persistently prayed for, and sometimes doubted finally arrived. They received a child and became a family. Their joy knew no bounds.

That was five years ago. Now they're sitting in my office casting barbs at each other. What happened?

Usually there are two sides to every story—*his* and *hers*. But in this rare case, Peter and Deb saw it the same:

Somewhere along the way we got so caught up in being the three of us that we lost the two of us. We had waited so long to be parents—to be a family. And when it finally happened, we just threw ourselves into the roles of Mom and Dad.

For the last five years, our lives have been so consumed with Megan that we've lost each other. Now we wonder if it's too late to get us back.

An At-Risk Group

This book is not about adoption. Nor is it about the unique problems faced by adoptive couples. It's about *ministry marriages*. Still, I've included this story to act as a metaphor and to illustrate an underlying theme that you'll find throughout this entire book:

Though it's true that every couple is unique and different from all other couples, it's also true that some couples can be grouped together according to their common features and common challenges.

This is the case with adoptive couples. Years of disappointment and anxious anticipation make couples like Peter and Deb vulnerable. As a group, they're at risk because once their dream of becoming a family is finally realized, they're uniquely susceptible to becoming *over*-involved in their roles as parents and *under*-involved in their roles as spouses. They're at risk to emotionally disconnect as a couple.

My describing the plight of adoptive couples hasn't been an attempt to educate you about adoption. Rather, it has been to clarify what it means to be at risk. Though the shared features describing what clergy couples have in common is very different from those describing adoptive couples, the diagnosis is the same. *Clergy marriages have a specific set of challenges that uniquely place them at risk.* These unique challenges are often overlooked.

The Teflon Mentality

In the more than 25 years that I've been a therapist, I have had opportunities to work in both secular and Christian settings and with Christian and non-Christian clients. Though there are a lot of positive things to be said about Christians versus their non-Christian counterparts, I've noticed one theme that's not so positive. Christians tend to see themselves as a little less human than non-Christians—and a little less susceptible to common pitfalls. Somehow we believe that our position in Christ exempts us from the frailties that normally befall the rest of humanity. I refer to this as the Teflon mentality.

You're familiar with Teflon. It's a miraculous product—especially for someone who cooks the way I do. Nothing sticks to it. Everything just slides off.

Teflon may work well with pots and pans, but the events of life don't simply slide off you and me. Though boundless resources are available to us in Christ, we're nevertheless human. The problems and pitfalls that can create havoc in the lives of non-Christians can be problematic in our lives as well.

What does it look like when someone exhibits a Teflon mentality? Something like this:

- What? Infidelity in my marriage? Never!
- What? Separation or divorce? No chance!
- What? My love for my spouse could dwindle and die? Impossible!

The truth is, I've seen spouses betrayed, marriages crumble, and love die. And I've seen it happen to Christians. What's more, I've seen it all happen to *ministry marriages*—the elite of the elite. Time and time again I've heard, "I never thought this could happen to me."

Much of this book is devoted to identifying the factors that uniquely challenge ministry couples—the things that put you at risk. But before you can benefit from recognizing the things that make you special, you must accept the reality that "if something can happen to *anybody,* it can happen to *me.*" No individual or couple is exempt. Teflon coats pots and pans—not people.

A Look at the Facts

For several years I worked with a telephone ministry to parsonage families. Pastors and their spouses were encouraged to call a toll-free number and speak confidentially with a professional counselor about any needs or concerns they might be having. Though this program was referred to as a crisis line for clergy, it really wasn't anticipated that pastors would be calling with a lot of crises—personal or otherwise. Rather, it was thought that most of the calls would be of a consultative nature. For instance, a pastor might call if he needed some professional advice about how best to deal with a particular counseling situation. Or he might have a church member who needed to be referred for counseling and be unaware of the availability of Christian professionals in his area.

Were we ever wrong! As anticipated, we did receive requests for consultation. And we did receive requests for referral sources. But these accounted for only a small portion of our total calls. We were surprised with the number of *stress* calls that we received from pastors and exactly what was stressing them out. Even more surprising was the number of calls we received from pastors' wives—and the reasons for these calls.

I was personally involved with this ministry for 10 years. During that time, the frequency of calls and the reasons for the calls re-

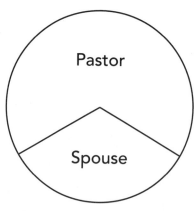

DIAGRAM 2.1—WHO CALLED

mained fairly constant from year to year. For every 1,000 calls, we found the following:

Breakdown of calls by *caller:*
- Two-thirds were from a *pastor.*
- One-third were from a *pastor's wife.*

When we started the crisis line ministry, we really had no way of predicting just how many pastors would actually call us. We knew the need existed, but we also knew it could be easy to find a reason to not pick up the phone, even though the call was confidential.

But the phone *did* ring—a lot. As mentioned, our greatest surprise was with the number of calls we received from the wives in these parsonages. As illustrated in the previous diagram, one call out of every three came from a wife. But we were also surprised with *why* these pastors and wives were calling.

Breakdown of calls by category of call from *pastors:*
- One-third were for *referral and consultation.*
- One-third were for *ministry stress.*
- One-third were for *marital stress.*

DIAGRAM 2.2—WHY PASTORS CALLED

We did get calls from pastors seeking *consultation* for some of the counseling they were doing and even an occasional request for a referral source. But these types of requests accounted for barely one-third of the pastoral calls. The remainder (two out of every three from pastors) regarded *personal stress* that the pastor himself was experiencing. These stress calls fell equally into two groupings.

The stressed pastor was feeling pressure either in his *ministry* (conflict with church members, board, or supervisor; difficulty meeting job expectations; disillusionment with ministry; being underpaid; spiritual fatigue; moral lapse; and so on) or his *marriage* (dissatisfaction, conflict, lack of affection, and so on).

Breakdown of calls by category from *pastor's wives*:
- One-half were for stress regarding their *role* as a pastor's wife.
- One-half of the calls were for *marital stress*.

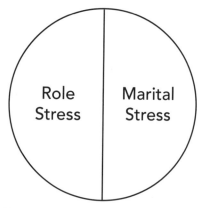

DIAGRAM 2.3—WHY SPOUSES CALLED

Unlike the calls from their pastor-husbands, the calls we received from wives were related to *stress* of some kind. Though we received an occasional call about problems with children, these were miniscule compared to the primary reasons for calls. Year after year, the same overwhelming pattern emerged. When wives called, either they were stressed over *their role as a ministry mate,* or they were stressed over *what was happening or not happening in their marriage.* Whenever I picked up the phone and was greeted by a woman's voice, I knew the conversation was very likely going to be about one of these two problems.

Reality's What *Is*—Not Necessarily What We *Want* It to Be

Jan and I were cotherapists with a group of clergy couples whose lives were in crisis. They had come from all across the country and from a number of denominations. The only things these couples really shared in common were a history of prominence in ministry (they had been the cream of church leaders), and a fall.

Kathy—I knew Gary was feeling some pressure from the church. He had grown quiet at home—even more quiet than usual. There was a time when I might have asked him what was wrong. But those days were long gone. I had long since grown accustomed to the emotional distance between us and just chalked up that part of our marriage as an unavoidable part of being in ministry.

At no time did I think our marriage was in trouble. Why should I? Gary was the senior pastor of the largest church in the state. We were doing God's work. We were where everyone else aspired to be. What could happen to us? Then it all came crashing down. *I never dreamed anything like that could happen to us.* Others, maybe. But not us.

Gary—Kathy had no way of knowing what I was feeling. I don't even think *I* knew what I was feeling. That's part of why we're here now—at least, that's why *I'm* here. I still don't know what happened.

Probably a bigger question than *what* is *how?* I mean, I did all the things I was supposed to do—committed my life to God, got the right education, served on the right committees, took the right churches. And all of this worked. I was at the top of the ministerial food chain. But somewhere along the way I lost my passion for ministry—and for Kathy. Then I did some pretty stupid things. *It isn't supposed to be this way.* I just don't understand.

Gary and Kathy were attempting to put their lives—and their marriage—back together. As therapy progressed, they made great strides in doing both. But what struck me most about their story was neither their challenges nor their decisions. What surprised me was their *perception* of reality. Each knew that things were not right, but each also thought that calamity would somehow escape them. Why? Because they were *special.* What sometimes happened to others did not happen to them. But it *did* happen—and their world came crashing down.

Embracing Reality

Being an at-risk couple is not a death sentence. It does not mean you're predestined to end up in a certain state or condition. It *does* mean that you can count on certain very identifiable factors to challenge your marriage—that *some things just go with the territory.* As a couple, you can choose to deny this reality. You can refuse to face facts, insist your relationship is special, and determine to exempt yourselves from the problems others face. Or you can choose to *accept* reality. Recognize that *being in ministry has its own set of unique challenges* for you as individuals and as a couple—challenges to be recognized, faced, and resolved.

This book is written for those of you who are willing to see yourselves and your marriages as vulnerable. It's our belief that when ministry spouses begin to truly recognize reality for what it is—not what they wish it were—they can work together to achieve the marriage that God intends for them to have.

We serve a powerful God who has boundless provisions and urgently desires to partner with us. It's when we see ourselves for who we are, and Him for who He is, that our marriages can thrive in a glass house.

His Life

Pastors Talk About the Challenges of Ministry and Their Effects on Marriage

We've heard from many pastors through the years of ministry and counseling. Not all their experiences are the same, and not all have been negative. After all, there's something special about being in ministry. But we've heard enough of the negative with enough consistency to be able to identify some common themes regarding the challenges of ministry and how they affect marriages.

These common themes—the corporate voice of pastors—will be the focus of the next four chapters. To no one's surprise, each of these chapters will deal with the stress of pastoral ministry, but each with a different look. In each instance, we'll explore the implications for clergy marriages.

We've learned of these themes in statements from pastors. Their experiences may be different from yours, and their comments may be different from yours. But both the experiences and the comments have occurred so frequently that we consider them common.

3

Donald Harvey

I'm Stressed

I t was my first counseling session with Sam and Donna. I knew they were in ministry, and I knew an affair had occurred. But that's all I knew. Being aware of very few of the circumstances that bring a couple to counseling is nothing new for me. I actually prefer it that way so that we can make their story the focus of the first session.

Sam and Donna had that ideal look about them. They were young, attractive, well dressed, and pleasant to be around. They had two small children to complete the appearance of the all-American family.

But looks can be deceiving. And based on why they were coming to see me, I knew there was far more to Sam and Donna than met the eye.

Sam did most of the talking, partly because of his comfort with communicating. Talking with others was not as easy for Donna. But Sam's tendency to talk in this first session was also due to his emotional state. He was in tremendous pain. Donna had betrayed the marriage, so it was only natural that Sam would still be dealing with the hurt associated with this betrayal.

But it wasn't that simple. In fact, Sam seemed to be less concerned with what Donna had done as with what *he* had done and what she might still do. He had a combination of guilt and fear.

Sam—We've talked more in the last couple of weeks than we have in the last two years. I've gone through a whole range of emotions—so has Donna. I think we're both settling down now. I didn't know for a while if we were going to make it. But some things have happened in the last few days to kind of turn the corner for us. Considering what we've been through, I think we're doing great. I don't know what's going to happen for us as far as our ministry is concerned. But I believe our marriage is going to make it.

I almost lost the most important thing in my life—my marriage. I feel like such a fool. All I want now is a chance. If Donna will hang with this thing, I know we can get things back to the way they were before I lost perspective.

I've worked a lot with infidelity. It's mind-boggling to see some of the choices that seemingly committed spouses make. But I've also seen enough to know that most affairs are symptomatic—they reveal something about the quality of the marriage that long preceded the act of betrayal. This statement is in no way meant to justify affairs. There's never a right reason for doing the wrong thing. But when we begin to see affairs as symptoms of something bigger, it helps us to understand and to rebuild. Based on the experiences I've had with other couples, I already knew that Sam and Donna's marriage hadn't been making it. And based on my knowledge of Sam's emotional state, I also knew that he was eager to explain just what had gone wrong.

Sam—Donna and I really had a great relationship before I entered the ministry. Wow! Even *saying* those words makes me feel as though I'm being blasphemous. It's sad to think that doing something so right could lead to something so wrong.

When we entered the ministry, we lost the romance. I'm not sure where it went, but I think losing it was closely tied to how Donna and I wanted people to view us. We wanted people to see us differently than we really are—to see us as *perfect*. After all, we're ministers, and ministers are special. We got so caught up in projecting this plastic image that we completely lost sight of who we really are. I guess losing touch was just the next step after losing sight.

Donna—I wasn't looking for another relationship when Chad and I got involved. I must have been really vulnerable at the time. I know I was really missing Sam. I remember telling Sam that I missed him so much that I ached inside. But it didn't do any good. He would act as if he were listening—but I knew he wasn't really. I had his eyes but not his mind. Sometimes he even made me feel guilty for wanting us to have a life. Slowly, the ache went away.

At the beginning, Chad and I were only friends. We talked a

little—but then we began to talk a lot. I remember feeling Chad really heard me and thinking just how long it had been since I had felt that Sam heard me. It was then that I began to realize just how much Sam and I had grown apart. The ministry had consumed him.

But I also realized how little I cared. There was a time when I cared a lot. But I guess being constantly ignored—telling Sam that it didn't seem we had any time for each other anymore, only to be discounted, put off, or attacked—had destroyed most of what I once felt for him.

The next thing I knew, Chad and I were commiserating about our marriages. I remember thinking, *This guy really cares about me.* It felt so good. I guess one thing just led to another.

Falsehood No. 1: "We Have to Be Perfect"

Part of the uniqueness of ministry is tied to the stresses that simply come with the territory. For the most part, the examples of stress that Gene and I will describe come from the outside—expectations that others place on us, keeping up with the demands of a changing society, and even from the role itself—the lack of privacy and some characteristics inherent in the title. But it was clear in conversation with Sam and Donna that the challenge confronting them came from an entirely different direction.

Sam suggested that his being in ministry had been hazardous to his and Donna's marital health. And that was true—it had indeed been stressful. But Sam's assessment was simplistic, and it would be inaccurate to merely say that ministry had been the culprit. It wasn't entering the ministry that caused their romance to depart—it was the lies that Sam and Donna brought with them. Their difficulty came from *inside* their relationship—not from anyone or anything else. They did it to themselves.

Sam and Donna illustrate a problem that challenges many ministry couples. It's the kind of problem resulting from what we believe and consequently what we tell ourselves. If what we believe is faulty, then we usually end up telling ourselves lies. That's exactly what Sam and Donna did. They told themselves a lie. They believed that as clergy they had to be perfect. So they got into the "role" of ministry. They assumed the look. They were going to be perfect instead of real, even if it killed them. In doing so they became plastic.

There's a real irony to Sam and Donna's situation. While trying to live by an erroneous standard, they were missing the true need of congregations worldwide. Congregations need leaders who aren't afraid to be real. Had Sam and Donna's belief been different—had they chosen the standard that says, "We don't have to be perfect, but rather with God's help we'll be real"—not only would their ministry have improved, but also their marriage would have been spared a lot of needless heartache.

This is not the only lie believed by people involved in full-time ministry. On a regular basis I find ministry couples experiencing needless stress due to two other falsehoods.

Falsehood No. 2: "It's OK to Put My Ministry Above My Marriage"

Remember how Donna ached for Sam—for some time and attention? She gathered up the courage and told him just how much she missed him. Yet he did nothing. Why? It wasn't that he didn't hear Donna's words. Somehow, Sam failed to hear her *heart*. He heard only words and then quickly dismissed them.

Donna was never able to get Sam's attention. She probably could have done something more dramatic than just talking to him. Maybe she could have gotten in his face, jumped up and down, or hollered and screamed. But even these extremes might have done no good. Sam never heard what Donna was really saying. He didn't realize the urgency of her feelings because he was telling himself another lie. Sam believed it was OK to put his ministry above his marriage because "nothing can happen to me or my marriage. I'm a pastor."

Believing that it's all right to put your ministry above your marriage is another example of buying into the Teflon mentality mentioned earlier. Sam was able to ignore Donna's words—and ignore her heart—because he believed he could safely operate with a different set of rules than those of people who were not in professional ministry. Somehow, God would protect his marriage in spite of his neglect, insensitivity, and its low priority. He was special. This Teflon mentality—the belief that "what sticks to others won't stick to me"—nearly cost Sam his marriage.

Just like the need to be perfect (or plastic), believing that you can live by a separate set of rules is a stress we put on ourselves. It may not feel stressful at the time. In fact, clinging to this lie probably brought Sam some relief. In his mind he could deal with the pressures of ministry without having to worry about what Donna was going to do. Nothing was going to change between the two of them. For that matter, nothing could change. They were invincible. And besides, he could always make things up to her later.

Think how reassuring this falsehood can be. "I can do anything without consequence." So if this lie is so calming, how does stress enter the picture? It usually takes a little while for stress to catch up. But this lie is a lot like sin. It always catches up with you. And when this cycle finally runs its course, as it did with Sam and Donna, stress hits like a sledgehammer. There's a reason why Scripture speaks of reaping what you sow (see Gal. 6:7-9). With this lie, stress comes with the reaping—not the sowing.

Falsehood No. 3: "I'm Not Supposed to Have a Life"

When others try to tell us in one way or another, "You're not supposed to have a life," we're looking at stress that comes from the *outside*. Gene will address this later. But when it's *us* making the statement—when we tell ourselves this lie—it becomes an *inside* stress. Here are some caricatures of people who see this as truth.

A Case of Guilt. For the guilt-ridden pastor, not having a life is an indication of true spirituality. "Sacrifice" is his "watchword and song." To do otherwise would mean to fall short of what God expects of him. Somewhere along the line, he has learned that *to do* is more important than *to be*. And even the thought that he might want to have some balance in his life is enough to cause him severe pangs of guilt: "If I haven't given up *everything*, I haven't given up *anything*."

This caricature reminds me of Matt. He and Sara came for counseling when the world as they knew it came crashing down around them. Matt had sacrificed everything in his life in order to give his all to ministry. This sacrifice had resulted in his climbing to the top of the denominational corporate ladder. But that all disappeared when he burned out.

Matt—I had been numb for quite a while. I would get up in the morning and go into the church, but I could only go through the motions of ministry. The passion was gone—and finally I just crashed. I didn't understand what was happening, and my confusion only made me angry at God: "I've given up so much—how could You let this happen to me?"

It's taken me a while to finally face the truth. Ministry wasn't about God at all—it was always about me. I had to measure up to this super-righteous role, or this incredible feeling of guilt would sweep over me. I wasn't spiritual enough unless I was . . . whatever. I just couldn't keep up the pace anymore.

It all had to do with *why* I did what I did. I was so messed up. Crashing was probably the best thing that ever happened to me. I see that now. My view of God is entirely different now—and I'm beginning to see *myself* differently too. Crashing is giving me a chance to get my life straight—to get some balance—and to finally do the *right things* for the *right reasons*.

A Case of Self-consciousness. For the self-conscious pastor, not having a life is an indication that he's doing an *adequate* job. Adequacy is a big issue. It is so big that he lets others decide whether he's measuring up or not. Somewhere along the line, he has learned that *to seem* is more important than *to be*. And whatever the cost, he's at least going to appear to be adequate (even though he never quite manages to feel that way). "What will others think if they see me taking a break? They might think I'm a slacker!"

This caricature reminds me of Dan and Kay. Dan had sacrificed almost everything in order to appear competent. He worked harder and longer than the rest of his staff—but apparently he didn't work smarter. The personnel committee met him at the church one morning and asked for his resignation.

Dan—I was crushed. No one gave more than I did. No one! How could I not be doing a good job? But they were right. I was so concerned with what others thought—everyone else—that I completely lost sight of the important things in ministry and the important things in life. I feel I'm learning some things about me that I've needed to learn for a long time. And I also believe that God's giving me a second chance.

Kay—We've been learning to laugh, and it feels so good. We talk now—really talk. You know—when you say words and the other person actually hears them. When you said, "God always has a future for His people," those words just resonated with my spirit. I really think He's going to do something special in our lives. Maybe we're just now getting to the place where He can really use us.

A Case of Piety. For the pious pastor, not having a life is an indication that he has achieved an *identity*. Like the Pharisees who received their reward on earth (see Matt. 6:16), sacrifice is all about identity—being identified as pious and saintly. And who's more saintly than a martyr? So not having a life is like wearing a badge. Somewhere along the line, he has learned that the most important thing in life is to be revered by those around him: "Nobody sacrifices more than I do. Look how much I'm giving up for the Lord."

This caricature reminds me of Dave. He had come from a meager background in every respect: socioeconomic, religious, and family. He had had little to give him any kind of start in life. Then, as a high school senior, he was exposed to the gospel and became a Christian. What a difference this made in his life! Everything changed for the good. But like some of the trips I've been on, not everything that starts well ends well.

Dave became active and involved in the church. Being new to the faith, he was like a dry sponge lapping up everything around him. His eagerness quickly landed him some speaking opportunities, and he was an instant success. Over the course of several years, Dave's success (and probably more the calling of the masses than that of the Lord) gradually pulled him from one ministry role to another until he had risen to astounding local prominence. A large church, civic connections, radio and television programs, the acclaim of the masses—Dave had it all, or so it appeared.

It felt good being at the top, especially on those occasions when he glanced back to see the place where his journey had begun. But this feeling was fleeting and quickly overshadowed by the nagging fear that one day he would be discovered for who he really was—a frightened little boy completely unworthy of love and acceptance. So Dave worked ever more diligently to keep up the facade. "If I give up enough, I'll be seen as special." This formula worked for over 20 years. But then came a crisis. And with the crisis, Dave and Linda sought help.

Dave—I told myself that my people needed an example to follow. I was to be their model of godly leadership. So when I was with them, I would put on my preacher voice. Even Linda and the kids knew the difference. It got to be a standing joke at home. I'd start to pray for one reason or another, and they'd shout, "Dad's putting on his preacher voice!"

I told myself that this was what I was supposed to do. But the truth is, it *felt so good* to have everyone look up to me, for them to see just how much I had given up for them and the calling of God on my life. I was afraid to let them see the real me. I didn't believe anyone could love me for who I was. And I couldn't stand the thought of losing what I had.

Linda—I never knew what Dave was going through. He never shared anything like that with me. He was always so dutiful, so responsible, so sacrificial. I thought he was so spiritual. I even felt convicted because I wasn't as spiritual as he was.

What this has taught me is that what our people need most is permission to be real. And there's no one in a better position to give this permission than the pastor. But it's going to take a pastor who feels good about not only himself but also his relationship with the Lord.

Challenging Our Beliefs

Cognitive therapists tell us that most of the distress we experience in our lives is directly related to what we tell ourselves. We have no one else to blame. They would further suggest that we challenge our beliefs to see if they're true. If we find them to be faulty, then we're to replace them with what *is* true. I personally think things are a little more complicated than most cognitive therapists believe. But I also think that what they suggest as solutions—challenging our thoughts—isn't a bad place to start when dealing with the stresses we put on ourselves.

Look at some of the things we tell ourselves, though not in so many words: "We have to be perfect." "It's OK to put my ministry above my marriage." "I'm not supposed to have a life." These three beliefs are guaranteed to stress us out. And they're lies. What would be more accurate? What's true? What would make your life better?

Sam and Donna have already helped us out with the falsehood. Instead of believing "We have to be perfect," they suggested that a truer statement would be "We don't have to be perfect, but with God's help, we'll be real." Wow! That sounds so truthful—and so freeing. Think of the stress reduction we would enjoy if we really believed that.

That brings us to the second falsehood: "It's OK to put my ministry above my marriage." I guess the simplest thing to do (though not very creative) would be to just insert "not" into the statement. "It's *not* OK to put my ministry above my marriage." If we believe that statement, think what that will mean for our marriages. But this belief will need the help of some companion statements to clarify and support it. For instance, "My most important relationship is with my God and Savior." "My second most important relationship is with my spouse." "Ministry, though a calling, is still 'a work' and is never to be so consuming that it unduly interferes with my responsibilities to my marriage." Believing these truths will help us appropriately prioritize the important things in our lives.

That third falsehood, "I'm not supposed to have a life," really speaks to the issue of balance. Removing "not" creates a statement that's truthful and freeing but also needs some support. Clarity comes with statements like "Healthy people have balance in their lives." "Healthy people base decisions on what they believe to be right instead of trying to please everyone else." "The Christian life is more about God and less about me." "*What* I do is important—but no more important than *why* I do it."

So how are you doing? Feeling stressed? Is any of it coming from the *inside,* from what you're telling yourself? Change begins with awareness. Take a few moments to honestly look at the beliefs controlling your life. And while you're at it, check out the effects of these beliefs. It may help to compare notes with your spouse. Sometimes others can see what's happening in our lives better than we can. And remember—you're both in this together.

4

Gene Williams

Everyone Has Expectations of Me

Y ou really are living in a glass house. And since your lives are so visible, some people feel inclined to correct you. Many of those you pastor feel they have the freedom to straighten you out in almost every area of your life. It may seem there's nothing out of the critic's reach. They see what they perceive to be a flaw and are determined to correct it.

Two of the most volatile objects of criticism are spouses and kids. I believe these flash points are targeted because they're such sensitive areas.

While I was pastoring a church in south Florida, my first wife, Bettye, who's now deceased, gave herself totally to ministry. We had five children at home—that was enough to keep anyone fully occupied. However, the church was short on developed leadership talent, so she began carrying several areas of ministry. She did not complain about her many responsibilities, although they created some hardship for her.

At one point she was teaching a growing adult Sunday School class, leading a weekday ladies' Bible study, and playing the organ for all services. She was not an accomplished organist but worked hard at improving until she became quite proficient. All of this took time and energy. She carried these ministries in addition to countless hours of counseling and the endless entertaining that goes with a growing church full of young families. She was all but fully employed by the church (albeit unpaid), and she still had five children and a husband who looked to her to be the heart of their home.

She strayed from a healthful diet and had no time for exercise and began to put on a few extra pounds. One of our dear members became incensed when one Sunday, as she moved from the organ to the altar to pray with someone, he noticed her dress was too tight. "She's wearing her clothes too tight and sexy!" he exclaimed. "Why isn't our pastor's wife more careful about her appearance?"

It was the same dress she had worn for two years before gaining the weight—and nothing had ever been said. Frankly, I wondered why he didn't offer to buy her some new clothes. I suppose it was easier to take a cheap shot.

Face It in Love

When the criticism filtered back to us, as it always does, we had to deal with it. We knew it could be a source of disturbance and division. Her decision was to let the problem be his. No, she didn't wear the dress again; one does not deliberately upset or offend. When possible, we keep everything on an even keel.

When there's no moral issue or biblical truth at stake, who cares? You may say, "But what about self-respect? Shouldn't I protect my rights?" Try to keep in mind that those who are sensitive to shallow issues will find their lives in constant turmoil. For many years I advised my staff that since we die only once, let's make sure we die for something worthwhile. Many pastors and spouses have gone to war over petty issues when they should have turned the other cheek. Every minister and every minister's spouse needs one blind eye and one deaf ear. See only half of what you think you see, and hear only half of what you think you hear! Take every criticism and cut it in half. In so doing, you'll defuse one of Satan's most destructive weapons—discouragement.

We who have been unfairly judged find ourselves in pretty good company. Not even Jesus was able to escape unfair, unjustified judgment. In Matt. 9:10-11, we read about Jesus eating with publicans and sinners. The religious leaders were livid, wondering how He could do such a thing and why He associated with such people. Sound familiar? If it hasn't happened to you yet, be assured: it will. Criticism is like death and taxes. It happens. Some folks take it upon themselves to correct the spiritual leader who they see as careless or less than perfect. It never crosses their minds to heed the words of Jesus found in Matt. 7:1-2—"Do not judge, or you too will be judged. . . . And with the measure you use, it will be measured to you."

Everyone I know needs forgiveness. Some critics have maneuvered themselves into a very precarious position with their judgmental attitudes. When the judgment they've leveled on God's anointed one comes home to them—and it will—they'll be very uncomfortable. God will watch over His faithful servants and apply the balm of healing to their wounded hearts. So let it be their problem, not yours.

Evaluate What You Hear

Are we to ignore criticism? Of course not. But we can take the stress out of it by genuinely looking at the charge. In some situations, we become better ministers by listening to the charge, evaluating it in a spirit of prayer, and then acting appropriately. Honestly ask yourself, "What is the spirit in which the criticism was given? Does this person love me? Is what he [she] said justified?" If it is, make the needed improvement, and thank God for making you more efficient. If it's not justified, thank God for the clearance of your character, and let it be the critic's problem. Truth will eventually come to the surface.

While pastoring in Gainesville, Florida, near the University of Florida, I was pleased to have a number of college students in my congregation. Some of them were graduate students almost as old as I was. I'm very grateful to one of those graduate students for making me a better minister. His name was Roy.

One Sunday as Roy left the service, he said, "Pastor, can I speak to you after everyone is gone?" I replied, "Of course." After the sanctuary cleared, I found Roy and asked what was on his mind. He said, "Pastor, I don't mean to be disrespectful, but this morning you said something, and I want to know where that is in the Bible." He proceeded to tell me what I had said and asked where it was located. I was on the spot. I knew it was in the Bible, but I didn't know where. Pride is not a problem with me, so I admitted to my friend that I didn't know where it was. Then I said, "I'll find it and tell you Wednesday night." And I did.

I also determined never to quote any statement from God's Word without knowing where it was. From that day on, I was very careful to document my notes with references.

That young college student put me on the hot seat. Should I have been upset, resenting his inquisition? Should I have felt pressured or stressed out because I had been confronted? Not on your life. He was justified in his confrontation, and he did it in a spirit of love. I owe Roy a debt of gratitude—he made me a better preacher and a better pastor. My temporary discomfort with his question has long since turned to joy in being a preacher of God's Word.

Often a Double Standard

Between the two of us, Joyce and I have seven children and 13 grandchildren, and there have been some potentially tense situations. Not all of my children have led saintly lives. In fact, there have been some very difficult times.

It's interesting to me that some laymen fail to give pastors' kids the same freedom to be kids that they give their own. When a pastor's kid gets out of line, everyone knows it. After all, they're supposed to be perfect. Not so with laypersons' kids. In some cases a double standard clearly exists. Recognize that for what it is.

After one such situation, God really helped me to see that while I was not vulnerable to many things, I was extremely sensitive about my children. So that's where Satan would attack. He worked on my weakest point and used innocent and well-meaning people to do so. Some of them never knew they were being used to create pressure.

Did the attack work? No. I determined to get closer to my children and to pray more for them. My critics helped me be a better father. I'm very pleased that as adults all of them are today serving the Lord.

This also made me realize that there are a lot of great laymen who reach out to help. Their love, support, and prayers have made a difference. While some were being used to create pressure, others were being used to take it off. Some felt free to gossip about every wrong thing the kids did. Others were supportive and complimentary of that which was right.

People Are Going to Tell You What They Think

Do we have to endure the pressure of criticism about ourselves and our loved ones? Jesus did. Is the servant greater than the Master? People will speak their minds. The next time you go to a ball game, listen. You'll hear criticism of the players, the coaches, and for sure the officials. Anytime you enter the spotlight of the public arena, you're fair game. Accept it. You don't have to like it—but accept it. Criticism is part of the territory. Is it justified? If so, let it guide you to make improvement.

What is the spirit in which the criticism is given? If it's given in harshness—such as with the man who criticized Bettye's clothes—consider the source. If it's in love, as Roy's was, thank God and improve. Some of my critics have turned out to be my greatest helpers. So will yours.

I'm sure you've heard the saying "No pain, no gain." Pain is sometimes necessary for personal growth. When you begin to feel the pain of the criticism—that which comes with the territory of a highly visible calling—determine to turn it into gain for the kingdom of God and for your own personal life.

I should be one of the strongest men in the world. I can hardly think of an area in my life that has not displeased someone. If I preached intellectually, I was over their heads. If I preached simpler messages, I failed to challenge their intellect. I finally decided to just be me—the best me I could be. But I was not and could not be the pulpiteer to compare with some of my peers. I determined early in my ministry that I would not allow lack of oratorical talent to ruin my life.

Know Yourself

I've discovered that my two greatest gifts are that of being a shepherd and of working hard. Fortunately for me, my father instilled a strong work ethic in me. So while I may not wow some with my pulpit oratory, I have earned some points in other areas.

I love to cook, so for 25 years I cooked for my entire congregation on Labor Day. I remember sweating profusely over a fish cooker one blazing hot September day. One of my church members came by and thanked me for what I was doing. He named one of the pastors whom I considered a great preacher and commented, "He could never do what you're doing!" He went on to add, "I sure do love to see you sweat! Thanks for the wonderful way you love us, Pastor!"

Having my children and grandchildren in the congregation has made me squirm more than once. My kids were not always perfectly behaved, and some members watched every move they made. I did wonder, however, how one vigilante knew that a couple of my grandkids were not closing their eyes during prayer. That was the charge: "His grandchildren's eyes are wide open all through prayer time." I know that keeping their eyes open was irreverent. I just wonder how she knew their eyes were open if her eyes were shut! So I took the criticism in that spirit. I won't buy into the double standard that expects more of preachers' kids or grandkids than laypersons' kids.

Until we recognize the source and identify who the enemy really is, these sorts of situations can really push the pressure buttons. In the case of the dear lady judging my grandchildren, she wasn't the enemy. She was the *tool* the enemy used to try to distract me from being the best pastor I could be to my congregation.

Did it hurt? Certainly. Did I enjoy the hot seat? Not at all. But recognizing the source and the spirit of a criticism helps you keep it in proper perspective.

Cooling Down the Furnace

There's a valuable old saying, "If you can't stand the heat, get out of the kitchen." Heat will come. In Daniel 3 the three young Hebrews—Shadrach, Meshach, and Abednego—teach all ministers a powerful lesson. Like every minister, they came under critical scrutiny. Their examiners watched to see if they would bow down to worship the golden image. When they failed to please the desires of their critics, the campaign was launched to eliminate them. Sound familiar? The scripture reads, "They neither serve your gods nor worship the image of gold you have set up" (v. 12).

The Hebrews examined the criticism. What their critics were saying was true, but they were clearly in God's will, and that came first. They chose to consider the source and realized that it was not coming from people who were in a good relationship with God. So they stood fast. When the pressure was on, they were given unwavering strength.

Look at verses 16-18:

Shadrach, Meshach and Abednego replied to the king, "O Nebuchadnezzar, we do not need to defend ourselves before you in this matter. If we are thrown into the blazing furnace, the God we serve is able to save us from it, and he will rescue us from your hand, O king. But even if he does not, we want you to know, O king, that we will not serve your gods or worship the image of gold you have set up."

The die was cast. The test was on. And what did they do? Nothing. There are times when we need to let God be our Defender. Oh, what peace is ours when we understand that! Just as King Jehoshaphat was told in 2 Chron. 20:15, "The battle is not yours, but God's." And He is a great defender of His people.

Do you remember what happened when the young Hebrews were thrown into the fiery furnace? "The fire had not harmed their bodies, nor was a hair of their heads singed. Their robes were not scorched, and there was no smell of smoke on them" (Dan. 3:27).

How much pressure do you think they felt the next time someone threatened them? Probably not much. They learned that while critics may cause trouble and discomfort, they cannot destroy God's faithful people. The trial by fire made them stronger than ever.

We'll be stronger, too, if we honestly examine ourselves in the light of the criticism and find ourselves innocent. You will become either bitter or better when you emerge from the fire. Once you survive the fiery furnace of pressure, you lose the fear of the heat.

When the Battle Becomes the Lord's

I determined not to let unfair, unjust criticism destroy my opportunity to serve God. I don't enjoy it, but neither do I fear it—I know what the outcome will be. As earthly parents don't eliminate all the problems from the lives of their children, neither does our Heavenly Father. But He's faithful to come to our aid and comfort.

A pastor friend of ours had faithfully walked through the valley of emotional trauma with Jim, a member of the church. As often is the case, new crises arose. After a year or two, the pastor became involved in helping others also, and Jim began complaining to anyone who would listen. In fact, he was successful in encouraging several of his friends to leave the church. He never went to his pastor to discuss the problem. Rather, he chose to go to others who shared his critical nature. He created such a fuss that the pastor, who had been faithful to the church for many years, eventually moved on to a friendlier environment. God said, "I have better things for you."

Jim's nature was such that no one identified him as the source of turmoil, and he was never held accountable by other members of the church. However, over the years "the Hound of heaven" made him very uncomfortable, and his conscience began to eat away at his peace of mind.

The funeral of a mutual friend brought Jim and the pastor and his wife together several years later. Jim's conscience could handle the guilt no longer. Tearfully, he asked his former pastor for forgiveness and received it. He could not stand the heat of the furnace into which he had thrust the pastor, a faithful servant of the Lord.

Neither the pastor nor his wife initiated this encounter—God did. He always enters the furnace with the faithful. That pastor and his wife were quick to forgive. God had given them a wonderful new assignment, and His blessings more than compensated for the difficulties they had experienced. The key to an enriching new life was in letting God fight the battle for them.

God has never lost a battle. If we let Him, He not only helps us survive but also enables us to soar to greater heights of confidence and joy.

Keep in mind that your critics may either be carnal or have good intentions. If they're carnal, just remember: so were Jesus' critics. If they're like Roy, my university student, they will help you become a better preacher of the gospel.

The stresses that come from others can drive the pastor and spouse apart or pull them closer together. Adversity builds character, and when it's faced together in God's presence, it builds the marriage relationship. You can be sure that the members of your congregation are aware of the pressure that you face. When they see the two of you face it together triumphantly, they take hope for the pressures in their own lives. So expect criticism to come, consider the source when it does, and pray for the hide of an elephant. You can become God's Exhibit A.

5

Gene Williams

It's Hard Keeping Up

H e came home from church that evening strung out from the pressure of the board meeting. She had spent her day in the parsonage wrestling with three small children. Both were worn out physically and emotionally. Between his tension and her fatigue, they hardly spoke to each other before they retired that night.

There was still a distinct coolness between them the next morning. In fact, it was only God's grace and their grit that allowed this stressed-out couple to maintain their marriage at all. They were living with pressure so intense that it was about to destroy their family. They were marital martyrs in God's service.

I'm happy to report their situation got better. Unfortunately, it was not a unique situation by any means. Far too often the outside stresses that affect us professionally come home with us. If pastors don't learn to adapt and adjust to these external pressures, they may find themselves bringing home unwelcome guests.

Ministry in the new millennium is in a constant state of change, and I hear pastors say, "It's hard keeping up." As an example of the changing landscape of ministry, look at what has taken place in buildings and styles of worship. During the 50 years I have had the privilege of being on God's pastoral team, I have seen churches go from small, musty basements with no amenities, to beautiful, well-appointed buildings with state-of-the-art equipment. Preaching in a basement church with a potbellied stove right in front of the pulpit, with your congregation sitting on homemade benches, has its unique challenges. On the other hand, standing in the pulpit of a sanctuary that seats over 1,000 on cushioned pews backed by a 70-voice choir and an orchestra has something more to offer—*increased pressure on the pastor.*

When I went to that first church, I was the only person in the room with more than a grade school education. The people listened attentively to my messages and plans, which came to them as the voice of God. I don't remember but one conflict at that little church. As the congregation began to grow, one of the charter members took the floor during a board meeting and said, "I don't like the way things are going around here, and I resign." After she stomped out, some of the others said, "Pastor, thank you for not bowing down to her. She's been holding this church back for years." We went on to double our attendance that year. Those folks believed in and respected their pastor.

I challenged them, led them in worship, and did almost everything else that needed to be done—including opening and closing the church building, taking care of custodial duties, and on various occasions giving about half of the congregation rides to church. However, the sense of respect I enjoyed as pastor didn't end in that basement church. It continued for the next 30 years or more. I served a very strong church in southern Florida with a congregation of more than 500 who worshiped in a beautiful building. It was a very different situation, yet there, too, I experienced a special sense of pastor-people relationship.

Two entirely different congregations, but both respected their pastor. Both congregations had a special love for the person who stood in their pulpit, prayed at their bedsides, and led them in spiritual growth. Was I perfect? No, I made a lot of mistakes. But because of their innate love for me, they willingly overlooked my blunders.

Things are different today. I haven't changed—but our culture has. I've witnessed a change in attitude. The pastor once occupied a very special spot in the hearts and minds of the people; that made pastoring easier. For me that meant that sometimes they had more confidence in me than I deserved. But I was their pastor, and they honored the position.

Respect can no longer be taken for granted. At best, we can hope to earn it. But being suspect instead of honored has changed the rules for pastoral ministry, and it's also increased the pressure.

There's Been a Change

Perhaps one of the reasons for the loss of respect for ministers is the public disgrace and downfall of highly regarded pastors. With the increasing media exposure of the moral failures of those who had enjoyed very visible ministries, skepticism has crept across the land. And this suspicious, critical attitude is putting pressure on the hometown preacher.

I would be the first to say that all ministers should not have to share in the blame for the misdeeds of a few. Yet the pall of suspicion is there, and there sometimes seems to exist a presumption of wrong rather than the assumption of integrity. How do we deal with it? Can we deal with it?

Pressure No. 1: Relinquishing Total Control

One of the best ways I've discovered for dealing with it is to allow businesspersons to run the administrative aspects of the church so that I can focus on the ministry. The church, whatever its size, needs to follow the best of business practices. Church is no longer a Mom and Pop operation, and ministers are not necessarily gifted with great business minds. If you're not confident in this area, allow someone who *is* to take responsibility for it.

I know a minister whose wife thought she had the gift of finances. So when he became pastor of a sizable church that she perceived to be struggling in that area, she took it upon herself to straighten out the problem. She was a business major and took great pride in her knowledge and abilities. Difficulties arose because she approached the problem in a way that was demeaning to some successful laypersons in the congregation. Some of them owned rather large businesses. They were not the dummies the pastor's wife made them out to be. As it turned out, the struggle had nothing to do with the potential leadership of the board. It was a personality conflict. And with that struggle came tension. Need I tell you that this sizable church began to shrink as the atmosphere became uncomfortable for many? As you might have guessed, the pastor has long since left the pastorate. The inability to acknowledge mistakes and personal limitations can put a pastor under great pressure that may lead to a rapidly dissolving ministry.

I know of one highly successful pastor who met with his board and struck a clear agreement that they would handle the business affairs of the church and that he would handle the spiritual matters. When finances were short, it was not his problem. The laypeople bought into the concept of carrying that responsibility so the pastor would be relieved of this great burden. The pastor focused solely on ministry. Consequently, his church became one of the greatest congregations in the South.

One of the best things you can do as a pastor is to determine what you know and what you don't know. Stick with what you know, and then find someone with whom the other matters can be entrusted. Does that mean that you relinquish all concern in these areas? Absolutely not! What it does mean, however, is that you recognize that as your people become more educated and successful in the business world, they're able to carry on some of the business of the church that you no longer need to wrestle with. Learning to acknowledge this paradigm shift will enable you to escape the pressure of being a "little emperor."

Pressure No. 2: Diversity

Baby boomers, busters, generation Xers—all have different needs and interests. They wear different clothes, eat different foods, and, most important to you, like different styles of music! This volatile mix is creating open warfare in many congregations. Can you guess who's getting squeezed in the middle? The pastor, who's expected to keep everybody happy. How does a pastor please the older group who loves the old hymns and also pacify the younger generation who wants upbeat contemporary choruses? It's a fine line. The challenge is to help an aging group that has brought the church to its present status understand the opportunity to pass the faith on to those who will carry the torch and to help the younger generation respect and cherish the foundation their older counterparts have laid for them.

You won't make everyone happy. A pastor who thinks he has pleased everyone should take a fresh look at Jesus' words in Luke 6:26: "Woe to you when all men speak well of you." It is impossible to make everyone happy all the time.

In one church that I pastored we had a problem getting the temperature right for everyone. One gentleman constantly complained that the sanctuary was too hot. He all but demanded that I have the thermostat turned down. As he left church one Sunday, he informed me that since I would not do anything about the temperature, he would not be back.

A little lady sitting on the same side of the church very close to the complaining gentleman approached me with the comment, "I nearly froze this morning. Is there anything you can do to make it warmer?" It was a no-win situation. Pastors will find that it is virtually impossible to give everyone what he or she wants.

You won't be able to satisfy all the people all the time, and sometimes you'll feel pressure from opposite extremes. How do you handle these potentially stressful issues? In the first place, recognize that pleasing everyone is impossible. No one can do that. Not even Jesus. So don't allow yourself to succumb to that pressure.

In the situation I just mentioned, the first complainer did indeed leave the church. In fact, he took several like-minded friends with him to a cooler church. I don't like losing anyone. However, I refuse to let Satan put a guilt trip on me. I was not a failure. The problem was not my fault. It's simply impossible to adapt sound and temperature to accommodate everyone.

Extensive studies have been made in an attempt to determine what worship format works best for most people. I know it sounds simple, but from my perspective, whatever works best works best. That will probably mean giving each group—boomers, busters, and generation Xers—some of what they want. Then try to help each group gain an appreciation for the taste of others. However, the pastor must not let himself be squeezed to death in an attempt to make everyone happy. Let genuine love for your people serve as a shock absorber for the criticism that will inevitably come.

I was having dinner with a strong layperson at a very good church when the subject of preaching came up. This man was highly educated and successful in his business. I'll never forget the comment he made about his pastor: "My pastor can't preach his way out of a wet paper sack. But I don't care—he knows the names of my children, and he loves all of us. I can put up with poor preaching to be loved like that."

Wise is the pastor who learns to express genuine love for his people. They will come to believe that their pastor's love is more important than buildings, worship styles, preaching styles, or any of the other pressure points of the day.

Pressure No. 3: "We're Not in Kansas Anymore!"

The day when divorce was rare in the church is long gone. Studies indicate that divorce rates in the church closely parallel those outside of the church. What does a pastor do when two members who are married to each other decide to divorce? The pastor loves them both. How can he minister to both of them without getting caught in that vise grip?

It isn't easy. But it can be done.

One of the young couples I married came to that point in their lives. In light of Matt. 5:23-24—"If you are offering your gift at the altar and there remember that your brother has something against you, leave your gift there in front of the altar. First go and be reconciled to your brother; then come and offer your gift"—I don't see how two Christians can divorce without serious spiritual implications. But this particular couple was convinced that their differences were irreconcilable.

First, I assured them that God loved them and that I did too. We loved them both equally and therefore could not take sides. I urged them to consider counseling with a professional marriage therapist. When they hesitated because of the cost, I simply reminded them that counseling was considerably less expensive than divorce—both financially and emotionally.

My decision to recommend professional counseling may have been the wisest thing I did. It permitted me to maintain my role as their spiritual leader. There are times when we are wise enough to know our own limitations. Unfortunately, that couple did proceed with their divorce. One of them eventually went to another congregation when the atmosphere became uncomfortable in our church, but we remained friends. Both of them still needed a pastor, and to this day they call me "Pastor," along with the members of their extended family.

Another area of potential problems is the business world. As I said concerning divorce, this should ideally not be a problem in the Christian world. But in this high-tech, fast-moving age, not all business deals are clean and simple. As a result, it can be scary when someone asks, "Is ——— a member of your congregation?" You recognize that the person he or she is asking about is a business leader and that the inquirer is a customer or employee. I have said on several such occasions, "Yes, but I don't know much about his business." And I've sometimes had to add, "I'm sorry you had a bad experience with that person." I've never approached the accused to straighten things out. After all, fools rush in where angels fear to tread. Since there are usually two sides to every issue, wise is the pastor who is not caught up trying to dispense the wisdom of Solomon.

Pressure No. 4: The Bottom Drops Out

A woman once came to my study and began to pour out her heart about one of my members. They had been sexually involved, and her conscience was eating her alive. He had been at the church for many years before I came as pastor, so he was well ingrained in the congregation. To make matters worse, he was on our staff!

I asked her to put everything in writing and sign it. This step was crucial, because she could well change her mind or story. I then asked one of my board members to meet with the accused and me. When we had gathered, I simply said, "I have a letter stating that you've had an improper relationship with a member of this congregation." He responded, "I know who it is, and it's true."

Since he was a member of our staff, I informed him that I expected his resignation and would leave it to him to explain as much or as little as he wanted to his family and friends. I insistently urged him to seek joint counseling with his wife. My heart would not allow me to publicly expose his situation. Because of that decision, I took some heat from the rumor mill. However, I was vindicated later when he confessed his guilt.

Fortunately, his wife stayed with him, and they had intense counseling. Later, his wife told me that the counselor asked her husband once what he thought of me and the way I had handled the situation. I wouldn't take anything for his response. He said, "He treated me like a Christian gentleman."

Some members of the congregation had only bits and pieces of the story, and I took a lot of criticism. Frankly, my wife was upset by the way I was treated. In the long run, though, the grace of God vindicated me.

Grace Changes Things

To say that this is a sensitive area of consideration would be a gross understatement. Moral failure in the Church is at record levels. The sad reality is that the ugliness so prevalent in our society has now invaded the Church. Add to that the fact that the divorce rate in the Church is very close to that of the non-Christian world, and you have the twin terrors of potential pressure for every pastor.

The tough dilemma is how to deal with the issue without destroying the people. In my early days of pastoring, we drew hard, in-

flexible lines. Sometimes we forgot that the Church is in the re-
demption business. If we're not redemptive in today's world, we ex-
clude innumerable people "at the well" from the love of God. Because the Church is called to exemplify God's love and grace, we
must open the arms of forgiveness. Neither moral failure nor divorce is unforgivable.

I believe the pastor and church can address moral issues without compromising the standards of the Kingdom. We'll be more like
Jesus, who looked at a woman caught in the very act of adultery and
asked, "'Woman, where are they? Has no one condemned you?' 'No
one, sir,' she said. 'Then neither do I condemn you,' Jesus declared.
'Go now and leave your life of sin'" (John 8:10-11). He did not excuse; He forgave. He offered help for a serious problem.

So must we! These twin terrors of divorce and infidelity are
tragedies of humanity. We recognize them as such and offer God's
healing grace.

Pressure Is to Be Expected

Pressures will come. You can be sure of that. However, if what we
preach is true, God's grace will enable us to survive and go on. I be-
lieve the key to survival is simple:
- Accept that you're not all-wise, all-knowing, or all-mighty.
- Recognize what you don't know.
- Listen to laypersons on business matters, and give serious
  consideration to their input.
- Listen to God on spiritual issues.
- Don't allow yourself to be caught in the vise of choosing sides
  unless serious moral issues are at stake.

Most pastors I know have great difficulty keeping the pressures of
the ministry from affecting the pleasure of their homes. That's why it's
crucial that pastors learn that some areas of ministry exist in which
they'll please most of their people—but probably not all of them.
Learn when to draw your line in the sand. Then leave it and go home
to love the members of your primary mission field—your family!

Your greatest success as a pastor is communicating genuine love
for your family. And while not all our children will respond as we
wish they would, they'll always know that, like the prodigal son, the
light is always on. There is a place of love and refuge—the presence
of the pastoral parent.

6

Donald Harvey

It Can Be a Lonely Business

I wasn't raised to fish, but I enjoy fishing. It's been more of an acquired taste. I've acquired a taste for other things Southern, like grits, turnip greens, and corn bread. But fishing has just about risen to the top of my list, and I've discovered something very startling about my new favorite hobby: you can fish just about anywhere! So whenever I travel—whether for business or pleasure—my first thought is "I wonder if I can fish while I'm there."

I was going to Dallas on one of those business-and-hope-to-be-fishing trips. So I called up a ministry friend to see if there would be any chance of our slipping away for a day. If so, I would bring some equipment. If not, I would travel light. Brad likes to fish about as much as I do. I knew that if there were a way to fit it in, he would do it. I was in luck. He had the time.

It was a warm summer afternoon, and we welcomed any breeze that came our way. We were fishing in a boat that the members of Brad's congregations had given him. They understood the pressures of ministry and the need to renew the soul. And for Brad, fishing was rejuvenating. He commented, "Even Jesus had times when He just had to pull himself away from the masses—though I don't know that He ever went bass fishing." Brad always had a good sense of humor, and he chuckled as he threw another cast at some unsuspecting fish.

There's more to fishing than catching fish. It's a process—one that can be refreshing, relaxing, challenging, and tiring all at the same time. But when you're with the right partner, it can also be enriching. Brad was one of those right partners: genuine, open, compassionate—the fellowship was every bit as good as the fishing. In between the fishing stories and our hi-tech discussions of all the new baits on the market, we began to talk about the pressures of ministry. This led Brad to make an observation: "You know, some of the pressures are easier to see than others." He went on to tell me about something that happened to him several months earlier.

Brad had taken a group of men from his church on a working retreat, one of those where you try to do it all: work, plan, and get refreshed all at the same time. In the middle of one of their planning sessions, Brad suggested that they take a break from the work phase and spend some time in prayer. So they all kneeled, and several of the men randomly led out in prayer.

After several minutes and sensing that it was time to bring their prayer to a close, Brad began to pray for each of the men individually. He called out each man's name and was able to cite specific needs that he was aware of. Brad then concluded his prayer and was beginning to rise when one of the men observed that everyone in the room had been prayed for except Brad—their pastor. "I want us to pray for you, Pastor." Brad was touched by Tom's concern and resumed kneeling. The men then all gathered around Brad, and Tom led in prayer. Brad later shared with me, "You know, it really meant something for Tom and the others to care enough about *me* and what *I* was experiencing to completely switch roles. They recognized that I, too, had needs—and they wanted to minister to me.

"But what really got to me was something Tom said in the middle of his prayer. I'll never forget it: 'And, Lord, bless *the keeper of secrets.*' Something in that phrase really touched me. I began to sob uncontrollably. Tom wasn't referring to any secret of his that I was keeping. But somehow he understood even better than I did the tremendous burden that goes with knowing so much—so much heartache, so much pain, so much contradiction.

"Knowing all this stuff and not being able to share a word of it is isolating. I *was* the keeper of secrets. And the pressure was greater than even I realized. I didn't know just how alone I had become."

I've Got a Secret!

Brad wasn't referring to his being a keeper of secrets as an isolated occurrence—no one had recently told him a secret that was weighing him down. He had found keeping secrets to be a pervasive part of his life. But neither was Brad describing something that only he experienced. No, he was sharing one of the realities of ministry. Keeping secrets is a part of the role; it goes with the territory. And it can create enormous pressure.

At times pastoring can be a lonely business, and one of the primary factors contributing to this sense of loneliness is the process of psychic isolation—having to constantly keep the important areas of your life under wraps. Secret keeping is a part of this process, but only a part. There are other ways to become psychically isolated. For example, look at how you relate to people. You interact, all right—but is it really you? In a sense, you're operating with a governor on your engine. By design, your relationships are supposed to be one-way. It's a role thing. You give, and they receive—and this direction is seldom reversed. Somewhere between your humanity and the application of this role requirement, your personal concerns get sacrificed. Seldom is it the real you that gets heard. It's just not the proper order of things.

Then there's the matter of those natural responses that you now keep in check. You behaved differently in your earlier life—before you entered the ministry. But those earlier days were carefree. You're in the real world now. You have responsibilities for others, and they're your greatest concern. Shock, elation, grief, sadness, anger—these are the things that used to be spontaneous. But spontaneity has become less and less a part of your life. It's no longer really acceptable. Now everything is calculated. You mentally screen your responses through your appropriateness grid. Your people's needs become your overriding concern. And what's the cost of subduing your natural responses? Psychic isolation—as you become further and further removed from who you are. Ministry can be a lonely business.

Where'd Everybody Go?

Also adding to your sense of loneliness in ministry is the sheer physical separation that goes with the job. Remember college and seminary—the bantering with classmates over the finer points of theology, the impromptu intellectual discussions over lunch, the stimulating philosophical debates over what effective ministry really looks like? Where did all those people go? Much like Dorothy in *The Wizard of Oz*, "I have a feeling we're not in Kansas anymore, Toto." You and your classmates left academia, and all went to different places. Now you're alone.

One of the greatest challenges faced by a therapist in private practice is combating the sense of physical isolation that comes from not having contact with peers. Sure, he or she may see several clients during the day. And some people will wonder how in the world a therapist can feel lonely. It's simple. Being with clients and being with peers are two different things. With clients, the therapist is performing a professional role—that of the giver while the client is the receiver. Conducting therapy can be fulfilling work—but it can also be lonely. For the therapist who has a solo practice, this lack of collegial involvement is like being stranded on a desert island. This feeling of relational deprivation is no different than that experienced by many pastors.

Another aspect of physical separation has to do with the work setting itself. When lay members of a growing congregation come to church, they find the setting is anything but peaceful. Pews are packed with people, sanctuaries are alive with music and song, classrooms are filled with busy children. Church is a sea of clambering humanity. But drop by on Tuesday morning or Thursday afternoon. You can hear a pin drop. As one pastor remarked to me, "The silence is deafening." This is especially true in smaller churches with little or no staff. A large empty building, even though a church, is still a large empty building. And it can be a very lonely place.

Do I Look like the Energizer Bunny?

Over the past several years I've had the opportunity to become increasingly involved in professional conferences. I guess that's one of the few perks of age. It's fairly typical for me to conduct a pre-conference seminar before the conference officially begins and then give a plenary address and present a couple of workshops during the conference. One thing that I've learned from these experiences is that there's a lot of difference between attending a conference and being a presenter at one. Being a presenter is far more demanding. I know that may sound obvious. Certainly there's more work involved in presenting than attending. But what I've found is that the presenting itself really isn't what's so demanding. I'm used to that, and I enjoy it a lot. It's everything *else* that goes with the role of being a presenter that kicks the intensity up a notch.

Whenever I'm a presenter, I'm "on" for the entire conference—not just the half-dozen hours or so when I'm behind a podium. I am constantly talking to people—before, during, and after my presentation. Sometimes people want to talk about the books I've written.

Sometimes they want to talk about the things I've said in the workshops. Sometimes they just want to consult with me about clients they're seeing in therapy. I understand this all goes with the territory, and I enjoy every minute of it. But it *is* draining. From the moment my airplane arrives until I take off for home, I'm *on*.

Following a three-day conference in Detroit, I had intentionally booked an early-morning flight so I would be home in time for Jan to pick me up at the airport and make it to the worship service at church. Following the service, Garnet came up to Jan and me and asked if we wanted to go out to lunch with him and his wife. Garnet and Lana are easy to be with. We've been friends for a long time, and none of us puts on airs. What you see is what you get. So lunch with them sounded good. Then he added, *"We have a group* going over to Germantown." All of a sudden the prospects for lunch felt different.

One of the best things about being good friends is that you can be completely honest. "You know, Garnet, I've just spent three days with the masses, and my emotional batteries are drained. I think I'll need to be recharged before I can be good company—at least with a group of people. Why don't we just take a rain check on lunch and do it some other time?" Garnet and Lana understood, and Jan and I dined alone.

Not everyone is affected in the same manner by experiences with the masses. My response is actually more typical of those with an introverted nature. I love going to professional conferences and speaking to therapists about therapy. I'm at that age where I'm trying to pass on some of what I've learned. I also enjoy conducting marriage enrichment experiences in churches and speaking at relationship seminars on university campuses. But these experiences always come with a cost. They exhaust me! An extrovert would have a different reaction. He or she would find mixing with the masses energizing—at least for a while. In time, however, even the extrovert begins to tire of always being "on."

Whether introverted or extroverted, the advantage I have over a pastor is that I can more easily withdraw from these demands when I need to. I can come home and get back to a different lifestyle. This option is rarely available to a pastor—or for that matter, a pastor's spouse. By virtue of the role, you're constantly "on."

Somehow there needs to be gaps in our togetherness. At least, that's the model that Jesus taught. There were times when He just had to be alone, to get some space, to recharge His batteries. For us, failing to create some gaps may result in energy loss. The early signs of emotional fatigue aren't always easy to detect. We're too responsible to just stop everything we're doing. And there's a lot of stuff that keeps on happening just by going through the motions and staying active. But if your passion wanes, other areas of your life will be affected. Pastoring can be a lonely business.

Being in Ministry Is a Lot like Being a Run-on Sentence

Jan and I were reading a book on prayer together. You know how it works—one reads, the other listens, and then you each talk about what it means to you. On this night Jan was doing the reading and I was doing the listening. After only a few pages, she abruptly stopped reading, put the book down, and said in a very exasperated tone, "I don't know how in the world this book ever got past an editor. That entire paragraph was only one sentence. One!" Jan is more adept at picking up on stuff like that than I am.

We then discussed the book for a while. We talked about what we thought the author was trying to say and how she was trying to say it. We finally agreed that neither one of us had any problem with the content of the book. In fact, it really touched us. Our problem was with her style—how she chose to convey it. *What* and *how* are two very different issues. We concluded that she didn't need to change any of the words. She only needed to add some punctuation. The book was "punctuationally" challenged.

Sometimes being in ministry is a lot like being a run-on sentence. We're so busy, so constantly giving, and so forever "on" that we inadvertently disconnect from meaningful contact—from the very thing that rejuvenates our soul. We become isolated. In these instances, the content of our lives may be OK, but we lack punctuation. When our lives need punctuating, we usually need involvement with people who have skin and bone and hair just like us. We can't rejuvenate on our own. We really do need each other.

Taking Self-care Seriously

Some of the stress of ministry is simply a by-product of the role. This is the case with isolation. What do you do if you want to prevent isolation from creeping into your life? What do you do if you want to reverse the isolation you're already experiencing? The answer is the same for both questions. You take control of the relationship balance of your life.

Doing this will require you to look at the four types of relationships that currently exist in your life. If each of these is already working for you, then your goal is simply to maintain what you already have. On the other hand, if they aren't, then your goal is to create them.

Develop Relationships with a Support Network

A support network is a group of people who genuinely care about you—those who allow you to be both a giver and a receiver. Some of these people can be like you—fellow ministry people. But some also need to be different, maybe from other denominations and entirely different walks of life. Have a support network of businessmen, plumbers, teachers, and so on. Expand your horizons. Seek relationships with those who need something you have to give and who can give you something you need.

Cultivate Relationships with a Chosen Few Confidants

While there can be several in your support network, only a select few will fill the role of confidant. This is your inner circle made up of people with whom you can and will share anything. And they know they can do the same. Confidants are your defense against *psychic isolation*. You can share your secrets. Of course, you protect the people who have confided in you by not disclosing identifiable information. But much like the therapist who seeks consultation from other professionals, you're able to process the content of what you know. Choose trustworthy people for your inner circle. If you feel your potential confidant is not completely trustworthy, look elsewhere.

Nurture Your Relationship with Your Spouse

Your relationship with your spouse is crucial and is your lifeline. Don't think that you can neglect it just because you have all these other relationships in place. A healthy marriage is a balance of *his, hers,* and *theirs.* He does *his* thing; she does *her* thing; and they do *their* thing. If the "their thing" isn't happening, every other area of your life will be affected. We invest in the lives of those who are important to us. This investment is both quantitative and qualitative. *Quantitative* refers to the amount of time you give to your marriage, while *qualitative* refers to the depth of the relationship. Do you and your spouse talk about what's really going on in your lives and the things that really matter—your fears, your joys, your dreams, your frustrations? Are you feeling distant from your spouse? Then look at the amount of time and the quality of time you're investing in your marriage. This is one area in which a little change can result in great improvement.

Protect Your Relationship with the Lord

When you're busy doing good—and working for the Lord usually qualifies as doing good—you can be tempted to let your personal devotional life slide. After all, everything you do is spiritually connected—it's God's business. And you're getting busier and busier doing more and more of it. It's easy to let the *doing* replace the *being*. Guard against the pitfall of proximity, in which being close to godly action is substituted for being close to God. This is a subtle way to lose your passion and to begin the descent toward isolation and loneliness. Guard your heart and stay connected. Nurture intimacy with God by protecting your time with Him.

Isolation and Marriage—a Final Thought

I debated how to approach my final thought on the isolation sometimes associated with ministry. I have no substantiating research to support my suspicions—only my experiences with clergy marriages in crisis and the experiences of fellow therapists who also work with clergy couples. But in my opinion, I can't express strongly enough the danger and far-reaching consequences potentially associated with the problem of pastoral isolation. It's been my experience that there exists a strong connection between clergy marriages brought to crisis by moral failure and those brought to crisis by isolation in ministry.

Depending upon whose definition you're using, moral failure can include a multitude of sins and activities. It's not my intent to define the term—only to point out that whenever I encounter problems with pornography, inappropriate Internet-maintained relationships, infidelity, or sexual addiction, the pastor invariably has been experiencing an enormous sense of isolation. Feeling completely alone and emotionally disconnected from all meaningful relationships, he errantly reaches out for something or someone to fill the void. The result can be disastrous.

We are relational beings created to be in healthy relationships with God and with others. When this is not happening, we're missing out on God's design for our lives and placing ourselves in harm's way. The potential for isolation in ministry is very real. It goes with the territory, but you can do something about it. Choose to stay connected.

Her Life

Spouses Talk About the Challenges of Ministry and Their Effects on Marriage

This is a book about ministry and ministry marriages. Remember: two spouses live in the glass house, not just one. We've identified many of the stresses of the pastorate and how they affect marriage. Now let's hear from the other half of the marriage relationship. These spouses did not all have the same concerns, and we heard a lot of good things regarding ministry and marriage. But we can identify some common themes of concern.

These common themes will be the focus of the next three chapters. Though each chapter is unique and addresses a different challenge encountered by the wives of those in ministry, a persistent thread ties them together. Each chapter is somehow associated to the role of ministry mate.

7

Donald Harvey

My Life Is Not My Own

A pastor I talked with recently said he had decided to change the focus of youth ministry in his church. "You know, we've had three different youth pastors in the last eight years, and they've all done a good job—but it's been the *same* job. I think we're ready for a little different kind of program." He went on to explain some of the things he wanted to see changed. He also said that he wanted someone more available to the girls in the youth group. "I think the girls have felt neglected the past few years. I'd like to have a couple so the wife could be actively involved in the ministry—someone for the girls to go to."

I thought about what he said for a few moments and then asked, "So are you planning to hire a couple?" He looked a little surprised at my question. "No! I'm not hiring a couple. I'm hiring a youth minister. But I want him to be married and for his wife to be willing to be involved as a *team.*"

As this pastor continued, it occurred to me that I had heard this story before, many times. But I had always heard it from the other side—from the spouse who was expected to be part of the team. I believe ministry can work as a team with both partners actively involved. But not all ministry couples have to work in this way. What this particular pastor was really talking about was the expectation of the roles—who was going to do what and why.

But this is also about control. From what I'm hearing, I believe a source of stress for clergy spouses is that when they are thrust into a role filled with the expectations of others, they feel they have very little to say about their own lives and ministries.

I recently met with a group of clergy couples who were discussing the inner workings of the church—staff assignments, who did what, how things really got done—which prompted one of the pastors to say, "You know, being a pastor's wife is a voluntary position." He thought he was being funny. But another pastor fired back, "Or an *in*-voluntary position." Part of the group laughed, but it was the kind of laugh that said, "Isn't that the truth?" rather than "That's really funny." Most of the spouses in the group weren't amused. They had experienced this thinking firsthand, and it had taken a toll on them personally as well as on their marriages.

Boundaries: *Who* Needs to Define *What*

"I feel like a baseball that's lost its cover—all my string is flying every which way." Judy's description of her life left little to the imagination. I understood exactly how she was feeling, and so did the rest of the group. Judy had come to Marble Retreat with her husband, Randy, to deal with the estrangement creeping into their marriage. As she spoke, it became clear that Judy's role as a pastor's wife was also an issue.

"My life is not my own," she said. "And as hard as I try, I can't seem to keep everybody happy." I asked her who decided exactly what her role in the church should be. Her response was revealing. "Randy, the elders, church members, and, of course, the leaders of our denomination—everyone but me." Most of the other spouses nodded in agreement. As diverse as their backgrounds were, these ministry wives shared a lot in common. Each was a partner in a deteriorating marriage, each felt tired and defeated, and each was experiencing feelings of lack of control over her own life.

Around the beginning of the second week, these ladies began to turn some emotional corners. Changes were taking place in their marriage relationships and in their personal lives. Many were reaching decisions about their roles—what they would and would not be and what they would and would not do.

Cindy began a morning group session describing how the elders of the church her husband pastored expected her to enroll in a computer course so she could organize administrative aspects of the church. This was just another in a long list of jobs assigned to this mother of three because she was the pastor's wife—duties no one else had the time or inclination to do.

Cindy decided she wasn't willing to give up time with her children to pursue the opportunity to become a computer whiz. She decided to listen more to God and less to the board.

Judy, who felt like a baseball without its cover, decided to make some changes as well: "I've been interested in the changes in technology for some time now, so I've decided to take a computer course," she commented. "I'm going to take charge of my life and do some things that are important to me rather than continue to let others tell me what I should be doing."

On the surface, it looked as if Judy and Cindy had made entirely opposite decisions. Judy decided to take a computer course, and Cindy decided not to. But each was redefining her role—based on what she believed to be right rather than what someone else thought she should do. Each was taking a step in establishing boundaries in her life.

These decisions will no doubt come with a price. Those who are accustomed to defining Cindy's and Judy's roles in ministry will be displeased. But once boundaries are in place, both Cindy and Judy will be more valuable tools for God to use in His service.

What Are Spouses Saying?

Not every ministry spouse encounters the pressure of expectations that Judy and Cindy experienced. And not everyone facing this pressure responds by completely sacrificing self in an effort to please others. But it has become clear to me that when others determine what the role of the pastor's wife will be, it creates tension for her personally and within her marriage.

I've dealt with this issue in our crisis telephone ministry for clergy couples. Fifty percent of the calls from pastors' wives—one in every two—concerned the stress she was experiencing in her role as ministry mate. I also encounter these concerns at conferences and retreats and sometimes when I'm pulled aside for an unscheduled consultation. The recurring theme is "My life is not my own."

Normal Is a *Range*—Not a *Point*

Confusion often exists regarding the spouse's role in ministry. The problem won't be solved by me or someone else coming up with a job description of what the spouse ought to do. Rather, it's a question of who determines what the spouse's role will be. And that decision ultimately rests with the spouse herself.

There are, of course, obvious parameters. We're to love God and seek His will in our lives. We're to love our spouses as we invest in our marriages and support our mates. But these are broad principles for guidance, and there are no specific goals that apply to everyone. What constitutes *normal* responsibilities for a pastor's wife is best viewed as a *range*. When *normal* is viewed as a *range*, we discover there's a lot of wiggle room when it comes to defining what's acceptable behavior and what's not.

← Extreme   (Normal *Range*)   Extreme →

DIAGRAM 7.1—NORMALITY CONTINUUM

What's right for one ministry spouse is not necessarily right for another. Different individuals have different strengths and weaknesses to draw from. They'll have different interests and passions, and they'll differ in where they feel called to invest their time and energy. They'll also be serving in churches that have different needs. All these factors need to be taken into consideration as a wife determines what her role will be. And a cookie-cutter mind-set in which everyone is expected to do things one specific way will only short-circuit the process.

Determine what you believe the Lord is asking you to do and be. As you rely solely on Him and grow in your role as ministry spouse, He will guide and sustain you and guard you from ministry spouse burnout.

Spousal Dictate

Remember Judy and Randy? When I asked her who determined what her role in the church would be, Randy was at the top of her list:

"Randy is like everyone else in my life. He's always got a plan for me—knows what I should do—and never hesitates to tell me! Sometimes I feel as if I married my dad, because most of the time he sure acts a whole lot more like a father to me than he does a husband."

Judy is describing a marriage with an imbalance in power. Randy has more to say about what happens in the marriage than Judy does. He isn't abusive. He doesn't humiliate or berate his wife. He doesn't intimidate, threaten, or physically strike her. But he exerts control over her behavior. He instructs her in what she should do instead of asking her if she would be willing to do it. And he expects her to automatically comply with his job description of what her role should be. He doesn't recognize that Judy may have her own opinion as to what her role should be. We call this *spousal dictate*.

Randy isn't totally to blame for the imbalance of power. The truth is, it was news to him. Judy had never told him she was unhappy with this inequity. She was trying to be a good pastor's wife and keep everybody happy. In her mind, speaking her mind constituted complaining. But how could Randy make changes if he didn't know there was a problem?

As it turned out, Randy was very willing to make adjustments in their relationship. But their marriage reached a crisis point before they talked it through.

How does spousal dictate affect a marriage? It creates an increasingly widening wedge between the spouses. The wife's resentment leads to resistance or perhaps outright revolt. This is especially true in cases in which there have been attempts to deal with the dissatisfaction but these efforts were in vain. The pastor-husband continued to do more of the same. If the spouse keeps her concerns to herself and suffers in silence, she simply becomes depressed. This is not what God intended for our marriages.

Spousal Nonsupport

Remember when Cindy decided to spend more time with her children instead of becoming the church's computer whiz? Her situation is a good example of *spousal nonsupport*. The computer situation was a new incident—but there had been others that preceded it. On a few occasions, Cindy had tried to establish some sort of personal boundary by doing something other than what she was expected to do. In every instance, her husband had failed to be supportive.

"The only thing I could count on was for him to not support me," she said. "He wasn't dictatorial or anything like that—he didn't tell me that I had to do it. But he wasn't supportive either. He would keep telling me to try to see it from their perspective. 'What do you think they will say?' 'They're not going to like it.' I think he was more concerned with everybody else's feelings than he was with mine. I just got to the point where I didn't even try anymore. What was the use? Just go along to get along."

In many ways, *spousal nonsupport* affects marriages similarly to *spousal dictate*. But with nonsupport we see more of a sense of disconnection. Spouses experience a greater sense of hurt and disappointment. They feel abandoned by the person they love. And they begin to lose respect. This can be devastating to the relationship.

No Cookie-Cutter Solutions—Only Benchmarks

There's no cookie-cutter job description here. Not everyone's the same. But there are some principles for health, concepts that will give guidance when you find your life is not your own.

It's OK to Think Outside the Box

Sometimes ministry couples limit their friends and activities to church. This can be stifling. When you look at taking charge of your life, "thinking outside the box" merely suggests that it's OK to establish a life that extends beyond the confines of the local church.

We begin thinking outside the box by changing our view of *people* and *activities*. Include people in your support network who do not go to your church—or who aren't even from your denomination. A funny thing happens when we step outside our denominational walls—we stop talking about religion and start talking about Jesus and what He is doing in our lives. That can be refreshing. And when selecting activities that you are doing for yourself, do not limit your alternatives to only those offered by the church. There are a lot of healthy activities that are found outside the walls of the sanctuary.

You Can Define Your Own Role in Ministry

We're not called to meet everybody else's expectations. Jesus couldn't accomplish this, nor did He try. Instead, He went about doing *the Father's* business (see Luke 4:43). That's the call on each of our lives—to do the Father's business—and the model we need to follow.

When I say that you can define your own role in ministry, I'm not suggesting that these decisions are to be completely autonomous. I believe that, as Christians, all our decisions should be made with the ultimate goal of pleasing God and in an attempt to know and follow His will for our lives.

In a real sense, our lives are not our own. Focus on your Creator, and let Him guide you as to how your life of service should be lived.

Seek Consensus Regarding Your Role as a Ministry Mate

Don't let defining your role as a ministry mate become a divisive point in your marriage. As a rule of thumb, any significant decision in your marriage should be made by both of you, including decisions concerning ministry roles. You and your spouse should come to a consensus.

Consensus involves two people who are willing to speak honestly from the heart, hear the heart of the other, and be willing to give up always getting his or her own way. That's a pretty tall order, but not impossible.

Being in consensus is more important than the issue you're trying to agree on. And for ministry couples, it definitely eliminates some elements of marital stress. Remember *spousal dictate* and *spousal nonsupport?* Being in consensus eliminates these.

Gaining consensus is a sign of a healthy relationship. Healthy spouses are able to dialogue about the significant issues in their marriage—and these interactions will lead to consensus decisions. Though not the quickest form of decision making, it's the best. If consensus decisions seem to be beyond you, ask yourselves, "Why is this so difficult for us?" If you still fail to resolve your issues, seek help to resolve your difficulty. It will be well worth your effort.

8

Gene Williams

I'm in Competition with the Ministry

W here have you been? I've been trying to reach you all afternoon! This has been one of the worst days of my life, and I couldn't even find you!"

To say my wife was upset would be an understatement. While I was out doing my ministry, she had faced a tragic situation alone. One of the ladies attending her Tuesday morning Bible study had suffered a heart attack and died in our living room. My wife had faced the mental and emotional trauma alone.

Frankly, she struggled with my being absent and unavailable during such a trying time. She felt she was in competition for my strength and help in her time of need, and she resented it. When she needed me most, I was nowhere to be found.

That day I determined to do everything possible to eliminate her feeling of competing for my attention. I purchased a pager the next day. From that time on, my wife could reach me instantly.

There's no way to avoid emergencies and other interruptions of our personal lives. What mattered to my wife is that I acknowledged her as a priority and that I never wanted to be out of her reach again.

I don't believe we need to live in an either-or relationship. Our families and our calling need not be in competition. We can achieve a balance and give proper attention to both these critical areas.

Mixing Marriage and Ministry Is a Critical Balancing Act

I remember watching in amazement as a man juggled four large, sharp knives in the air. Juggling several balls or bowling pins is one thing, but those knives could do serious damage.

As I watched him, I noticed his incredible concentration. His mind and eyes focused completely on the handles of the knives. He finished without a scratch, with not a drop of blood. The onlookers breathed a collective sigh of relief.

That incident reminded me of an interview with a high-wire artist I saw once. He was asked how he managed to maintain his balance on such a small wire so high above the ground. His reply was classic. He said, "I focus on the wire and never take my eyes from it." He paused and then added, very firmly, "Never!"

These two experiences remind me of the lifestyle that exists between a pastor and his wife. Whether you're juggling ministry and marriage or concentrating on staying on a high wire, both require attention and commitment. Many will be watching to see how you pull it off. Will the pastor rise to the challenge of two very demanding relationships—with his marriage partner and with God? To do so, he must determine early on that successfully mixing these highly demanding callings will not happen by accident.

Facing the Issue

Every pastor must feel called into the ministry. It has been said that if no overwhelming, impossible-to-ignore conviction compels a minister to enter this holy office, he had better not touch it. Paul expressed the calling in 1 Cor. 9:16—"I feel compelled to do it. Woe is me if I do not preach the glad tidings [gospel]" (author's paraphrase).

This call is a complete commitment of time, energy, and involvement. Foolish is the person who chooses ministry as a profession and fails to face up to the emotional and physical demands it requires. During the 50 years of my ministry, I have reminded God many times that ministry was His idea, not mine. And since it originated with Him, I was leaning on Him to provide the wisdom, energy, and resources needed to carry out the calling. If we choose ministry of our own accord, we will be dependent on our own resources. No one wants that. What a difference it makes when we're committed to leaning on Him and following His plan in our ministry!

Still, the pastor-minister must learn how to juggle this demanding call with family responsibilities that are just as challenging. In chapter 2 Don spoke of the "Teflon mentality"—the idea that human problems slide off divinely called people. This misconception exists with many ministers and is nowhere more obvious than in the marriage relationship. Every married pastor is living with a very human person complete with all of the physical and emotional dynamics that we all manifest. How do we mix the demands of a divine call within the human relationship?

Scores of times in the retreats for pastors and wives that Joyce and I lead, wives approach her about their frustrations of being a pastor's wife. Some of the most frequent phrases she hears are "I feel as though the ministry is my husband's alone. We don't share it." "I'm a pastoral widow." "My husband never does anything with the kids and me." "He's never home." "We never talk. He listens to everybody else but me." Sadly, these complaints are often justified.

In order to be successful at the juggling act of marriage and ministry, one must make a conscious decision to have a biblically based marriage and to keep that commitment in our minds at all times. We can choose to let our minds work in our favor or against us. There's too much at stake to take that chance.

Peace Provided

It's God's provision that enables the minister to be the spouse God requires, and relying on Him brings great mental peace and emotional rest. Operating on your own provision places you at risk for unbearable pressure—pressure that will likely affect your relationship with your spouse.

It's easy to become obsessed with solving the problems of our ministry and the church. What will it take to keep everyone happy? Where will the money come from to finance the programs? How can the youth ministry be strengthened? Who will teach the classes? The tension is a volcano waiting to erupt. But the minister whom God has called has a resource for help and insight. God takes care of the needs of His Church. The peace this knowledge brings will give you a sense of quietness, and this quietness will allow you to hear your wife's voice.

Taking Responsibility

"He listens to everyone but me." Remember that most common complaint? Then we have its counterpart: "He has time for everyone but me and the kids." In marriages in which these complaints are justified, the minister is making a major mistake—he's missing the biblical standard. And he can't blame that on the call of God.

I've spent many hours counseling men who have made hunting, fishing, or golfing widows of their wives. While there's certainly nothing wrong with those hobbies, the husband has a biblical mandate to make his spouse a priority. This also applies to pastors who make their wives ministry widows.

Pam seemed to have no special call on her life, but her husband, Dan, did, and she loved him. He was gifted, bright, charismatic, and a successful pastor. But he became so absorbed in his ministry that Pam felt she was on the outside looking in. The resentment she harbored because she felt she was vying for his attention began to elbow out her love for him. Ultimately she began to see his ministry as his mistress. Their three children, their extended family, Dan's career, and the congregation all paid a heavy price when their marriage fell apart.

How can this sort of ministry-marriage disaster be prevented? I've listed some ideas to help you communicate to your wife that you hear her and that she's a priority in your life.

- Take time for at least one date each week. This could be lunch or dinner out. Even if it's something as simple as a walk together, don't let anything less than a major emergency interrupt your plans. It's important that the two of you set aside time to look each other in the eye and communicate.
- Give your free time to your family. If possible, make Saturday your day off so you can be home when your wife and children are at home.
- Make special days special—birthdays, anniversaries, graduations, whatever. This lets your family know that each one of them is special to you and always in your heart.
- From time to time, bring home flowers, even a single rose or carnation, for no reason at all. There's no better way to say, "I'm busy, but you're always on my mind."

A Loaded Situation

The mother of small children sometimes feels she spends her whole day talking to little ones. The highlight of her day is when her husband arrives home and she can enjoy conversation with a grown-up. True, her husband has likely spent his day interacting with adults—some of them with adult problems—and he's physically and mentally weary. What he wants most is peace and quiet. This is a recipe for misunderstanding.

At the risk of oversimplifying the issue, let's look at Eph. 5:25, which says, "Husbands, love your wives, just as Christ loved the church and gave himself up for her." True, this is primarily pointing to the loving sacrifice that Jesus made for us. But it's also a call to express boundless love for our wives. I believe a parallel can be drawn from this selfless act of Christ to the selfless attitude of Christ.

Remember the encounter described in Mark 4? Jesus had spent an exhausting day ministering to many, and when He got into the boat, He quickly fell asleep. When a storm overtook them and the disciples needed Him, they cried, "Master, don't you care that we're sinking?" He did care, and He found the energy to meet that need.

Luke 18:15 is another example of the loving concern of Jesus. He had spent the day teaching, and the disciples saw His fatigue. They wanted Him to rest. Still, when mothers brought their children to Him, He found the energy to give them His undivided attention. Never did He claim "ministerial privilege" to excuse himself from loving relationships.

There come times when you arrive home exhausted but your wife needs your time and attention. Children get sick, the house gets messy, or you face other draining family situations. Find the strength to talk, to help with the children, and maybe to help in the kitchen or the laundry room. It speaks volumes to a weary wife when you put her needs and your family's needs before your own weariness and summon the strength to love her as Christ loved the Church.

Attention, Please!

Kingdom work is absorbing—there is always something pressing to be done. Sermons must be prepared, committee meetings must be attended, calls are waiting to be made, or a budget is in need of balancing. The average pastor works 60 to 65 hours each week on over 250 tasks. As the congregation grows, so does the workload.

With the Kingdom demands on your time, your wife sometimes tries to make do with the leftovers. And even when you're at home, your mind is often elsewhere. Your wife knows when she doesn't have your undivided attention, and this causes her to feel she must compete with your ministry for your time.

The truth is, she deserves more than your leftovers. You must consciously cultivate the art of emotional intimacy and meaningful conversation to preserve the fragile walls of your glass house.

Short but Sweet

Not all conversations need to be 30 or 60 minutes long to be meaningful. Pick up the phone during the day just to let your wife know you're thinking of her and that she's a priority in your life. An extended talk exploring deep thoughts is not necessary. Just making contact lets her know you love her and that she's important to you. Even making eye contact when you're in the pulpit and she's in the congregation speaks volumes. When life gets hectic and personal time is short, the memory of these stolen moments will help carry both of you through.

Busyness Breaks Hearts

He was handsome, talented, and successful in fulfilling his divine calling. He was considered an excellent preacher and was pastoring a growing church in the South. She was busy with four children who required a great deal of time and energy and the demands of being the wife of a dynamic pastor of a burgeoning congregation.

He was doing his best to be all things to all people. That meant early-morning breakfast meetings and late-night committee meetings. She rarely woke up to the warmth of his arms or enjoyed a meaningful conversation with him before she went to sleep.

When they did talk, it was mostly about how it would be better soon when things were under control. He thought she understood.

She didn't.

Soon she began to pour out her heart to a male parishioner who was eager to listen. It began very innocently. Her husband knew they were talking—there was no secret; nothing was hidden. In fact, he encouraged their friendship.

Nothing sexual developed between these two friends. But his emotional availability slowly drew her away from her negligent pastor-husband. Eventually it ceased to matter to her how much time her husband spent absorbed in his "good thing." She had found someone who looked into her eyes when she spoke and listened to her words and her heart. She quit competing for her husband's time and attention.

Divorce brought down the walls of their glass house. Four children suffered. A strong congregation bled. His ministry was destroyed. He had forgotten he wasn't just a pastor—he was a husband.

In God's eyes your marriage is a consuming commitment, as important as your call.

"Husbands, love your wives, just as Christ loved the church" (Eph. 5:25).

9

Gene Williams

When I Complain I Feel Guilty

G ood Christians never complain. Pastors and their spouses are good Christians. Therefore, pastors and spouses never complain.

Really? Who said so? I haven't been able to find that in the Bible. When did we modern-day believers achieve a higher level of grace than the disciples? Is the bar of expectation for pastoral families even higher than the biblical level?

In conferences at which I've spoken, I've heard scores of pastors and their spouses request prayer as they sought God's forgiveness for complaining. I'm not advocating whining when conditions are uncomfortable, but I believe we have biblical permission to register our displeasure. I would like to see the idea eliminated that pastors and their spouses forfeit their right to register complaints.

A Faulty Formula

The problem begins when one takes a fact and begins to draw conclusions that aren't true. One such example would be that since we're saved by grace and don't merit God's love (true), we have no right to complain about anything that happens in our lives (false). God's grace is wonderful, and I'm eternally grateful that He loved me and changed my life. However, I'm still a human being, with all of the feelings that go with being human. I still become disappointed with what happens to my humanity. When I'm disappointed, I'll register a complaint somewhere. God's grace is sufficient for every problem and pressure we face, but that does not mean we'll enjoy and take delight in them. It means He'll help us get through the moment.

Job was a blameless man, upright and reverently respectful of God. God referred to him as "my servant, Job." When calamity struck, however, this man in whom God had the utmost confidence became very unhappy, as we read in chapter 3. "May the day of my birth perish" (v. 3). "Why did I not perish at birth . . . ?" (v. 11). "I have no peace, no quietness; I have no rest, but only turmoil" (v. 26).

Job worked his way to 19:25-26—"I know that my Redeemer lives, and that in the end he will stand upon the earth. And after my skin has been destroyed, yet in my flesh I will see God." We also see this in 23:10—"But he knows the way that I take; when he has tested me, I will come forth as gold." However, we take note that even Job had difficult moments. And he *complained*—"Even today my complaint is bitter; his hand is heavy in spite of my groaning. If only I knew where to find him; if only I could go to his dwelling!" (23:2-3).

The point is, the idea that people who please God will never register complaint is a faulty formula. What pastor or pastor's spouse is greater in God's sight than Job? At times I've laid my case before him, as Job did in 23:4—"I would state my case before him and fill my mouth with arguments." My mouth has been filled with arguments. Believing that we must never complain is a tool Satan uses to create discouragement. We're imperfect human beings who hurt—and complain about it.

Your wife may feel guilty registering complaint about the unrealistic expectations of the congregation. Or she may feel guilty complaining about your marriage relationship.

Faulty Formulas Create Guilt

Were I to create a list of the faulty formulas used in creating guilt, it would look like the Book of Numbers. However, the victims of these faulty formulas are real people—wives of ministers who have lived with unfair and unbelievable expectations. These women, whose lives cease to be their own, are targets of Satan's guilt trips.

I have observed a multitude of pastoral spouses over the last 50 years, and each is unique. Let's compare just three.

WIFE A

I am by nature an introvert. My husband and I met at a Christian college, and we fell in love. Neither of us had a clue about living in a glass house, and those first lean years were a challenge. I soon discovered that I was the first layperson whom everyone, including my husband, turned to when something needed to be done. I was uncomfortable playing the piano, but that became my job. Soon I found myself coordinating Vacation Bible School, teaching the teens on Sunday mornings, and working as the church secretary.

As the load got heavier, I kept smiling, and everyone assumed I was content. At home I let my pastor-husband know that I was not happy with the demands placed on me. However, every time I complained, I felt enormous guilt, and I saw myself as a failure and an unsatisfactory pastor's wife.

When our first baby was born, I became even more stressed. The day my husband came home to find me soaked with tears and dirty diapers, he finally listened as I sobbed, "I just can't do this any longer!" He heard my words, and he heard my heart. He pulled me into his arms and told me I was going to take a "leave of absence." He explained to the congregation that they must pool their resources to fill the gaps while I took time off. I found my smile as I physically felt the guilt dissipate. And I never loved my husband more.

WIFE B

I've never met a stranger. When I fell in love with a quiet seminarian, it was a classic case of opposites attracting. We believed we could complete each other's lives. I loved his calm, peaceful demeanor. He envisioned my outgoing personality as an asset to his future ministry.

Our first pastoral assignment was a tiny church in a demanding parish where most of the members were elderly and accustomed to lengthy pastoral visits. Early on, I accompanied my husband on those visits, but soon I began to find them boring and repetitive. I taught the young adult Sunday School class and was soon asked to be choir director. It seemed I couldn't say no. More and more assignments came my way. Before either of us realized it, we were spending very little time together. I felt guilty about my unhappiness with my church duties, and my dissatisfaction was loud and clear as I expressed my complaints to my husband. He chose to turn a deaf ear. Sometimes when I noted his fatigue after a long day, I felt guilty about venting my frustrations. So I began to internalize my feelings.

After months of this pattern of noncommunication, I decided to get my real estate license and do something that I wanted to do. Before long, I tasted success. But I couldn't squelch the guilt, and as we grew further apart, I worked harder to find fulfillment.

After three years, I moved out of the parsonage and filed for divorce. In my farewell letter to my husband, I told him I just could not live with my failures and my guilt any longer. I felt nothing I did was good enough. I just wasn't cut out to be a pastor's wife.

It's essential for the pastor to listen and to affirm his companion. Legitimate complaints need to be addressed, and a wise pastor and husband will address problematic issues and help determine resolution.

Not a Blank Check

I'm not advocating a book of blank checks for complainers. We all know chronic whiners who are self-absorbed and for whom no amount of attention and praise is ever enough. Read on.

WIFE C

I was raised in an environment in which I was clearly the star. I had several brothers, but as far as my parents were concerned, the family revolved around me. I was spoiled.

I loved the attention and was greatly disappointed in situations in which I was not the main event. As I grew older, I became adept at manipulation and was very successful at getting people to do what I wanted. I married my high school sweetheart, and a few years later he was called into the ministry. I was delighted when the church became a stage for me and later for our daughter. We were the stars! If someone else was in the spotlight, I was unhappy and made everyone around me miserable. It was my idea, my way—or get out of the way!

My gifted and talented husband paid a heavy price. He was forced out of a strong, thriving church to move to a much smaller, struggling one—a church where there was no competition for our "marvelous talents." For years I made my complaints loud and clear and felt absolutely no guilt. No one dared question my opinions or criticize my self-absorption. I never intended to ruin my husband's ministry—I just did. Too late I realized that the problem was my attitude.

Aside from the transforming grace of God, there's little help for persons such as this. But every pastor's wife should feel free to register legitimate complaints without feeling guilty. To be able to say, "I don't like that," or "That makes me uncomfortable," is a God-given right. Don't feel guilty if you don't embrace every expectation or "opportunity" with open arms. Imitate Paul, and register discomfort with the problem while determining not to let guilt overwhelm you. God either removes the offending task or gives sustaining grace to fulfill it.

Ministry spouses are not superheroes who can do it all. Step back, take a deep breath, and be the best person you can be. God expects nothing more.

The Problem of Guilt at Home

Not all guilt trips come from the church. Many wives are struggling in their ministry marriages because they fail to understand that they're married to fallible human beings. While the call to the ministry is God's highest call, the individuals involved in the ministry are not perfect and are sometimes downright irritating.

If the ministry wife places her mate on a pedestal, she will experience a guilt trip every time she complains or disagrees. The following young lady went away to college feeling that God wanted her to marry a pastor. She was sure this would please God and assure her of a perfect husband. In her estimation, ministers were next to God. She soon discovered that her pastor-husband was only human:

I thought all my dreams were coming true when I met my husband. I admit it—I went to college looking for a preacher-husband. I found one, and we were married during our junior year. I dropped out of school and worked so that he could be a full-time student. I have never regretted marrying a minister, but I have learned some difficult lessons.

My husband serves God intensely, and he is absorbed in his ministry. Frankly, I think he should spend more time with the kids and me. I don't want to take him away from God's work, so I feel guilty when I try to talk to him about it. I don't want to be in competition with God, but it would be nice to have my husband's attention now and then. It's frustrating. I hope God understands and will forgive me.

Another wife put it this way:

I married a minister assuming he would remain the warm, loving, and understanding man I fell in love with. I elevated him to a level next to God. He turned out to be like everybody else. I hear other wives complain about being a golf widow or fishing widow. They complain openly about their unhappiness with being left alone. I feel guilty about expressing discontent with any aspect of my life. I'm a ministry widow, and I only get a few crumbs of my husband's time now and then. I don't like it, but when I try to talk to him about our relationship, I feel guilty—as if I'm asking him to be a bad pastor. Sometimes I feel I'm the enemy's ally.

Competition with the ministry—both of these wives are feeling the pinch. But we've already dealt with competition. This is about the guilt. A wife should not feel guilty for expressing her feelings of neglect and frustration.

Sometimes the congregation expects too much. Sometimes the minister-husband expects too much. I'm sure that at times I've been the one expecting too much. But I've learned that things change through open communication.

Guilt Creates Coolness

Satan wins when guilt wins. It's hard to be warm, loving, and responsive when you're feeling like a failure. Guilt trips are lonely journeys. I believe it's biblical to speak our minds to God without feeling guilty. After all, He made us to be emotional human beings. However, once we speak, we're obligated to listen for His answer.

The apostle Paul complained. Then he stopped to listen and heard such good news that his liability (a "thorn in the flesh") became an asset. With joy he shared God's words to him: "My grace is sufficient for you, for my power is made perfect in weakness" (2 Cor. 12:9). Paul goes on to comment, "That is why, for Christ's sake, I delight in weaknesses, in insults, in hardships, in persecutions, in difficulties. For when I am weak, then I am strong" (v. 10). May we learn to turn our thorns into triumphs!

Their Life
Couples Talk About the Challenges

In the previous two sections we've talked about *his* life in ministry and the stress associated with his call. And we've talked about *her* life as a ministry spouse and the pressure associated with that role. Now we'll concentrate on concerns that ministry couples typically have about their marriages.

Their experiences may not be the same as yours, and what they have to say may not be exactly what you would say. But both the experiences and comments have occurred so frequently that we consider them common.

10

Donald Harvey

We're Confused!
What's Marriage Supposed
to Look Like Anyway?

I answered the phone and heard not the typical "Hello. This is ———. How are you?" but rather these simple two words: "I'm scared."

Nothing else. And the caller didn't identify himself.

Taken off guard, I responded, "Why?"

He was calling anonymously from another part of the country. He had just received word that a close friend of his who was also a pastor had resigned from his church and left his wife and family for another woman.

"This is the fifth time in my 15 years of pastoral ministry that a colleague has left the church because of infidelity," he continued. "It scares me to think it could happen to me." Whether in the laity or the ministry, when a marriage is betrayed and falls apart, it's extremely hurtful to all involved.

I couldn't quite understand why my caller's response to this sad news caused him to feel afraid. Anger or grief seemed likely. But fear? So I began to ask him some questions to help me get at the heart of what he was feeling.

"Did you feel scared the first time you heard of a pastor-friend being involved in betrayal?" He took a moment to deliberate and then responded, "No."

"What about the second time you heard of this occurring?" Again his answer was no.

I then asked about the third and fourth times, and his answer was the same. This was the first time he felt afraid it might happen to him. I wondered what made this time different from the others. So I asked, "If you weren't scared in these previous incidents, why do you think you're scared now?"

"I don't know why it's so different this time. I'm just as surprised as you are. I just know that it's different. Right now I'm really bothered, and I don't know what to do about it."

My anonymous caller had told me nothing about his own marriage, and I wondered if learning a little about it might shed some light on his feelings. "Tell me about your marriage. What's it like?"

After a slight hesitation, he began. "It's OK. A little static, but it's not much different from most of the marriages around us. Should I expect it to be any different? I mean, we've been married for 17 years. I guess I don't expect it to be like it was when we first got married."

I sensed I was on the right track. I already knew the caller was confused by his emotions. And now he revealed that his confusion included marriage in general and his own marriage specifically. *Should I expect it to be any different?*

"Is Something Supposed to Be Happening Here?"

Jan and I have developed a retreat for couples that we call Marriage Enrichment Experience. We based it on a very simple philosophy: retreats should be fun and enriching. To meet these goals, we practice the three Rs—*relax, revive,* and *relate.* Relaxing is accomplished by planning some downtime in the schedule. All work and no play makes for a dull boy—it also makes for a dull retreat. Reviving, though somewhat tied to the content of the group sessions and the interaction between the couples, is really the result of the retreat as a whole. Relating is achieved through specially designed couples' tasks—exercises that encourage husbands and wives to privately discuss the things that are important to them.

We usually begin with one of these tasks—a nonthreatening marital pulse-taker that's completed at the close of our first group session. It's a brief questionnaire asking each spouse to answer five basic questions about his or her marriage.

This activity is more than just an icebreaker. It's designed to help couples take a look at how well they're doing in their marriages. Are things progressing well, or is there room for improvement?

When it comes to defining what marriage is all about—what's *supposed* to be happening—we get the big picture on pretty good authority. God gives us the design, and He does so in Scripture. With these questions, we're allowing husbands and wives, in a very tangible way, to ask themselves, "Are we growing our marriage God's way?"

The Big Picture for Marriage

We get the big picture for marriage in Genesis. After creating the heavens and the earth, vegetation, living creatures, and man and woman, God created what many describe as the first and most sacred institution—marriage. "Therefore a man shall leave his father and mother and be joined to his wife, and they shall become one flesh" (Gen. 2:24, NKJV).

The richness of this verse is often overlooked. This is God's biblical basics for marriage, and it's only when we delve into the intent of this passage—to grasp the richness of God's design—that we begin to absorb God's desire for marriage.

More than an Institution

Marriage enrichment experiences are designed to make good marriages better. At least, that's how we promote them. The underlying assumption is that most of the couples attending already have pretty good relationships. That's not always the way it works out, however.

An older couple approached me during a break at a recent retreat Jan and I led and said they wanted to talk privately about their marriage. They were eager to describe their 30 years of misery.

Fred—I haven't had a moment's peace since I married Sue. I can't do anything to please her. We just fight all the time.

Sue—I think Fred's number-one goal in life is to aggravate me. Whatever I want done, he's going to do the opposite. If I say "black," he says "white." He's pure meanness.

I thought they were going to start an argument right then and there. They weren't interested in marital advice—they wanted an audience. Each proceeded to tell me how bad the other was and how much of a cross he or she had to bear. Fred and Sue are classic weary warriors. From what I could see, their description of 30-plus years of misery was no exaggeration.

I'm always compelled to ask weary warriors at least one question: "As miserable as you are, what keeps you together?"

Fred and Sue's response was exactly what I've come to expect. "We don't believe in divorce, and we're committed to the marriage."

I'm reminded of a story I once heard about Ruth Bell Graham. She was asked in an interview if she would ever consider divorcing her husband, famous evangelist Billy Graham. "Absolutely not," she quickly replied. "I believe too much in the sanctity of marriage to ever do that. I might shoot him—but I'd never divorce him."

Both of these stories highlight a commitment to the *institution* of marriage. And although marriage as an institution is an accurate view, we miss the big picture if we fail to recognize that God created marriage to be a *relationship*. This dual nature of marriage is acknowledged in traditional wedding vows:

> Jack, will you have Jill to be your wedded wife, to live together after God's ordinance in the holy estate of matrimony? Will you love her, comfort her, cherish, honor, and keep her, in sickness and in health; and, forsaking all others, keep yourself only unto her, *so long as you both shall live?*

So long as you both shall live—these words express the time frame in which this institution is to exist. *Love, comfort, honor, cherish, keep, forsake all others*—these words speak to the *relationship*. My weary warriors had the institution down pretty well. They were in this thing for the long haul. But they were sorely lacking in the relationship department. There was no investment—no giving. There was only structure. They lacked a *dual* commitment.

A singular commitment to either the institution or the relationship is flawed. Commitment to marriage as only an institution is legalism. We all know what that produces. But commitment to marriage as only a relationship is just as bad. This attitude produces an unstable relationship, one that hinges on what feels good at the time.

Commitment to the institution of marriage offers security and stability. Commitment to the relationship provides the fertile soil where love, honor, and all those other good things can grow. The institution and the relationship work together to undergird a strong marriage.

Be Joined

I like to think of God as the first epigenetic theorist. "Epigenetic" is a term that refers to developmental stages. It suggests that there is an order to things—first you do this, and then you do that. The particular stages are identified in the order in which they're experienced, as are a unique set of tasks to be accomplished during each stage. It's important that tasks associated with a particular stage be completed before one moves on to the next stage.

God's design for marriage as given to us in Gen. 2:24 is a simple model with only two stages. The first is leaving home. Leaving is a process that isn't done in one step. More than geography is involved. Just because you've moved into a dorm room at college doesn't mean you've left home. And there's more involved than specific behaviors. Doing your own laundry doesn't mean that you've left home. Leaving home has to do with the emotional side of family relationships—dependency, decision making, and parental influence. The standard I use with university students is "Do the decisions you make have more to do with you or your parents?" Somewhere in the process of leaving home, young men and women are to make the break and begin depending on themselves financially and emotionally instead of their parents. They are then ready to go on to God's second stage—marriage.

The goal of the first stage is independence—to disengage from your family. The goal of the second stage is, simply stated, to join together to develop an intimate relationship—to become one flesh.

The second stage can be broken down into five substages to identify different challenges. For instance, we describe the stages of "married with young children" followed by "married with teenagers" followed by "married with grown children," and so on. All of this is intended to point out that we experience different demands depending on where we are in the process of life. And it's complementary to God's model, not contradictory. Whether it takes 5 stages or 55, the goal for marriage is to join together. As you move through the rest of your life, you're to be constantly working at becoming one flesh.

God's design for marriage is for us to join with our spouse: to draw close, to bond. That's it. Donald Joy indirectly spoke about this goal in his 1985 book *Bonding: Relationship in the Image of God.* Dr. Joy identified all of us as bonding beings and suggested that we're created for intimacy—vertically in our relationship to God and horizontally in our relationships to each other. We remain unfulfilled until these needs are met. Though Dr. Joy's book was not written to couples, the most intimate horizontal relationship we'll ever enter is the relationship with our spouse, the person with whom God has joined us. We're created for intimacy, for companionship, and marriage is designed to meet this need in our lives.

Back to My Anonymous Telephone Caller

We left off with my asking my anonymous caller about his own marriage and the confusion that this seemed to cause him. I went on to ask him how heavily he was investing in his marriage. It was as if I had just switched to a foreign language. After another long pause, he gave me another "I don't know." The funny thing about "I don't know" is that it usually isn't true. People generally know—they just don't want to talk about it. It's often used in an attempt to avoid answering a question and is not an honest indication of ignorance. So I persisted by asking him to describe a normal day.

"Well, let's use yesterday as an example," he said. "I started off by meeting a church member for coffee at six o'clock. By the time I finished all the things that I planned on doing during the day, including all of the unexpected things that came up, I finally got home just before midnight. Not every day goes like that, but a lot of days do. I knew ministry was going to be demanding before I ever became a pastor."

My instincts told me this caller had emotionally disconnected from his wife. I doubt it was intentional, but it had occurred nonetheless. The news about his friend came as a shock, but more than that, it caused him to be circumspect—to look at his own marriage. And what he saw scared him. Whether he wanted to admit it or not, at some level he knew something was missing. Intimacy may be something that's difficult to describe, but we generally know whether we've got it or not. When he realized something was missing, he realized he was vulnerable. I shared some of my thoughts with him:

> We've been talking quite a while about your situation, so let me make a few observations. First, I'm going to use a spiritual analogy to make a comment about marriage. Suppose you asked a church member, "How's your relationship with the Lord?" and he said, "It's OK. A little static—but it's not much different from most of those around me. Should I expect it to be any different? I mean, I've been a Christian for 17 years. I guess I shouldn't ex-

pect it to be like it was when I first got saved." How would you respond?

Would you think that this was fine—everything's OK? My guess is that you'd be concerned. You might even say it's time to have a revival or do something to break these people out of their complacency. And you'd think this because you realize that a relationship with God ought to be different after 17 years. It should be better—more intimate, deeper. Well, marriage is the same way. Sure, it's supposed to be different—but better, not worse. The relationship is supposed to be deeper and more intimate.

Second, your life is out of balance. One of the formulas for healthy relationships is *his, hers,* and *theirs.* He does *his* thing, she does *her* thing, and they do *their* thing. It doesn't sound as if much of *their* thing is happening for you and your wife. Ministry is demanding, but so are a lot of other things. The point is, do you allow these things to control your life, or do you control these things? The way you answer this question will determine if you're in balance or out of balance.

You're scared because you know there are some things missing in your marriage. Obviously, you're not happy with what you're discovering. But being scared is good. It's a wake-up call to change things.

We continued to talk a while, and he shared how things had started out differently for them and how and when things started to change. It's usually easier to look back and recognize the changes that have taken place than to see them in process. We then talked about the investments that build a relationship and what would need to happen if he was going to turn things around. The more we talked the clearer it became that he really wanted to regain what had been lost. He wasn't sure what intimacy was, but he knew he didn't have it.

Nothing "Just Happens"

When speaking of his wife, a friend of mine used to say, "I'm a better person because of Peg." I watched their marriage, and he was right. I saw how Peg helped Bob prioritize a demanding lifestyle and didn't allow anything to creep in between them. But Peg could have made the same statement. She was a better person because of Bob—and for the same reasons. They had mastered the formula.

There was definitely a *his*—Bob had a life. And there was definitely a *hers,* because Peg also had a life. But somehow in the demands upon his life and hers, they had managed not to neglect their life together. And that's the way it's meant to be.

Marital success or marital failure is not an event—it's a process. And intimate relationships are never accidental—they never just happen. If you have the kind of marriage you are created to have, it is because you've intended to have it and have made the effort to achieve it. Sure—we all have the occasional intimate experiences. These occur spontaneously and without planning, and they're nice when they occur. But an intimate relationship occurs only by design. You'll have to fight for it.

If you have an intimate relationship, you've placed boundaries in your life and carved out time for the two of you instead of placing everything and everybody ahead of your marriage. You've shared deeply, talking about dreams and fears instead of remaining safe and superficial. You've dealt with dissatisfactions as they arose instead of comfortably avoiding what may have resulted in conflict. And you've both listened and heard what the other had to say. If you're growing a marriage God's way, it's because you've done these things and more—because you also realize that nothing ever "just happens."

11

Donald Harvey

We Can't Seem to Fit Everything In

I'm really frustrated with my life! I don't even know why, much less what to do about it."

This was Paige's response to my first question of "What brings you in today?" She was confused and didn't know where to turn for help.

She seemed to have everything going for her: youth, energy, education, appearance, career, church, a good husband. But appearances can be deceiving.

"My husband, Phil, encouraged me to go talk to someone," she explained. "He knows I've been unhappy at work quite a while. He doesn't know if the problem is really with my job or if it's something else. And he doesn't really care what I decide to do. He just knows I've been pretty unhappy, and he doesn't want to see me hurt any longer. He's Mr. Supportive—and probably the greatest thing going on in my life right now."

Paige continued to talk and told me about the three years that she and Phil had been married. A lot of firsts had occurred. They entered their marriage as they were finishing college, so their wedding was followed with an immediate move from the cloister of a campus environment with student responsibilities to that of living in the real world. They also moved away from friends, family, and church for the first time to begin careers in a different area of the country. Phil entered the ministry, and Paige entered the business world. Both of them had to adjust to responsibilities far different from flipping burgers or cashiering at a local department store. But they had anticipated each of these firsts, and they enthusiastically embraced them. They saw them as good things, a rite of passage. Yet now, only a few years into the adult process, Paige found herself frustrated. And she wasn't sure why.

"I'm not doing well at work," she told me. "I know that's part of my problem—and that's mostly what Phil hears about. There's just so much to do there, and I can't seem to get it all done. My job performance is beginning to suffer, and that makes me feel bad.

"I think about quitting, and Phil's OK with that. He's OK with anything I decide to do. He says, 'It's your decision. Do whatever will make you happy.' But I don't know if my job's the real problem. Maybe it's me. If I were better organized—you know, worked smarter or maybe was more motivated—maybe I could get more done. I don't know. That's part of my frustration. I'm so confused. I don't know where to start. When it gets right down to it, I don't think I'm doing well in any area of my life."

Paige had everything going for her—or so it seemed. Actually, the more we talked, the clearer it became that having everything might be part of her problem—at least, *wanting* to have everything. Paige's statement that she wasn't doing well in any area of her life was descriptive and diagnostic as well.

She couldn't seem to give work what was needed in order to get on top of things and move her career forward. But that wasn't the only place where Paige was falling short. Church was the same story. She wanted to have an active part in Phil's ministry, and she did. But there were only so many hours in the day and still a great deal of work that needed to be done. And as if her expectations weren't enough, there always seemed to be others at church who had some pretty good ideas themselves about what her ministry ought to look like. The result was another area in which Paige was constantly feeling overwhelmed. And then there was home.

"You know, I love Phil, and I love spending time with him," she said. "But we just don't seem to be able to give each other what we need. Sometimes I feel that we're emotionally disconnecting. The times we're together seem to be focused more on relaxing than relating. I can't imagine what we would do if we had children. Between his life and mine, we can't handle what we've got going on now. We just can't seem to fit everything in."

Paige was stressed all right, but the real stress couldn't be blamed on her job. Nor could we fault the church or even Phil. And her problem wasn't going to be fixed by working smarter or improving her organizational skills. When you got down to it, she was driving herself crazy, the result of an errant value system. Sure, Paige needed to change some things in her life to reduce her stress. But before she could enact any long-term changes, she would first have to give up some of the lies controlling her life—lies that had come from the world in which she lived.

Recognizing the Difference Between *In* and *Of*

In John 17:15-16 we find Jesus praying that we should be *in* the world but not *of* the world. Usually when I think of this passage, it's in regard to questionable values and moral behavior. We live in a fallen world, and our ways are not the world's ways. For instance, as Christians we strive to be honest. But this is not always the world's way. The world says it's all right to sacrifice honesty at times, because sometimes being honest just isn't good business. The fact that others behave without integrity does not deter us, though. We recognize unscrupulous behavior for what it is, and we choose to live by a higher standard. Remember: we're *in* but not *of* the world.

However, when it comes to marriage, being in the world but not of the world takes on a different twist. It's not what the world has to say about morality—the bad things—that creates the most difficulty. We do a pretty good job deciphering between what's morally right and wrong. But it's when the world begins to speak about things that are perceived as good that we become vulnerable. It was the good things that challenged Paige—and it's the good things that will challenge you. These good things have become the challenge of the new millennium.

Joining seems like such a simple thing, but experience tells us that this is not the case. If joining were that easy, everyone would have an intimate marriage. Since so many couples do not, it must not be as easy as it appears. What is it that makes becoming one flesh such a difficult task? That's a hard question to answer. As individuals, we're complex, and so are our relationships. I could offer my opinion, but for any answer to be correct, it would need to be thorough, and this book is not intended to be a thorough treatise on marital health. Rather, it's intended specifically to look at clergy marriages and the stresses that ministry couples share in common. But if we were to look at a sampling of the interferences to our growing close—paying special attention to what's being said by clergy couples—at the top of my list would be the lies that the world tries to pass off as truths. And these lies often have to do with these good things.

Lie No. 1: You Can Have and Do It All

Paige seemed to have everything going for her, but she was still frustrated with her life. She felt she wasn't doing well in any area important to her. And she and Phil just couldn't fit everything in. Paige's problem was she was not only living *in* the world but also living *by* the world's standards. The world says, "You can have it all" and "You can do it all." You can have a demanding and successful career, an enriching marriage and family life, and a full and meaningful personal life outside of family and career. That's simply not true.

You can have a lot of one and little or none of the others. You can even have parts of it all. But you can't ever have it all. Paige was going to have to let go of the lie, the dream, and then she would have to restructure her life.

For Paige, it boiled down to priorities. She would need to make some choices and adjust her goals. Certainly, she could learn to work smarter—and that could help. But that wasn't the total solution. She also needed to schedule her priorities instead of prioritizing her schedule. Talk about proactive. That's life in a nutshell. Working smarter, as good as it sounds, is a way for us to prioritize our schedules. We keep pursuing the dream that we can somehow have it all. But letting some things go—recognizing that you can't really have it all and choosing to do the important instead of the urgent—we begin scheduling our priorities. This view of life, of course, directly challenges the value system of the world.

I once counseled a music minister and his wife whose marriage had been balanced before moving to Nashville. But when Steve joined the staff of a church in Music City, everything changed. The church demands were no different from what he and Janet had experienced before. But suddenly Steve found himself enticed to pursue a lifelong dream—a recording career. The hours were long and he was rarely home. When he was at home, he might as well not have been. "I have his body but not his heart," Janet said. There was nothing wrong with Steve pursuing a recording career. He was doing good things. But what about the cost to his marriage?

I remember waiting a few sessions before confronting the imbalance in his life. Finally, I felt the need to say something about priorities and the consequences that our behavior, whether through direct actions or neglect, can have on our marriages.

"You know, Steve, I understand your desire to follow your passion for music," I said to him. "But you seem to think that you can throw all of your energy into one dimension of your life and still have fullness in the others. That's not the way things work. A good marriage is going to cost you something—and right now you're giving it nothing."

Steve gave me a deer-in-the-headlights look. It was as if I was sharing breaking news with him. He truly thought he could have it all. But he was mistaken. They weren't able to fit everything in, and it was time for Steve to make some choices. Was he going to schedule his priorities, or was he going to continue in delusion?

It's always tough choosing between good things. What is it that is most important to you? Maybe you'll make a decision that's good for now but not forever. After all, circumstances change. Or maybe there are just some things in life that you'll never experience to the fullest. Maybe you'll let some dreams die—or at least modify them. Maybe you won't quite make it to the top of the corporate ladder, even if that ladder is in a denomination. Maybe you won't be the Martha Stewart of your neighborhood if you decide to tackle a career. Who knows what you'll decide? Just know that you'll have to make choices if you're going to have what you most desire in life. You can't have or do it all, and living by this illusion will result in your failing to do well in some or all areas—and you'll be continually frustrated. You just can't fit everything in.

Lie No. 2: Success Is a Legitimate Obsession

The second lie is more overt than the subtle belief that you can have or do it all. This lie has to do with success, something that has taken such a prized position in our society that families are being sacrificed without a second thought, because it has become legitimate to do so.

Technological advances are occurring at an exponential rate. Rather than making our work lives easier, we're working longer, harder, and with more stress. How did that happen?

Maybe things are changing so quickly that we just can't keep up.

Not only do I have to know my job, but now I must keep up with changes in the field that are occurring more rapidly along with technology. Thirty years ago, therapists didn't have to know about technology. Today we spend hours on our laptops learning systems that will be obsolete in two years. It's becoming more and more difficult to be successful—and more and more important that we are. At least, that's what the world tells us.

Clergy—the Same Obsession but with a Little Twist

Jan and I were counseling a group of clergy couples at Marble Retreat when one of the wives made a surprise announcement at the beginning of a morning group session: "We wives got together last night and figured out that the real problem is with the guys. So we've decided to go to Hawaii for the rest of the two weeks and let you work on them."

Stephanie's remark prompted some chuckling, and she intended it to be humorous—to a degree. But the group also perceived a hint of seriousness. Stephanie was alluding to the observations made by each of the spouses during the introductions on the first day—that their husbands seemed to be more interested in church success than marital success. After a little bantering, Wayne felt the need to respond to Stephanie's comment and defend the men: "You wives don't understand the subjective call of God upon our lives. We really have no choice. Ministry is a high calling. We are doing the Father's business—and that means there will be personal sacrifices."

I could see the potential for the group to slip into some nonproductive activity that would prevent them from dealing with what really brought them to Marble. They could end up debating theological issues and safely avoid the real reasons for abandoning their families. So I intervened: "You know, guys—these are philosophical issues. You could spend the remainder of your time here talking about these things and still not come up with good answers. But that's not why you're here. It would be more productive to look at what else may be influencing your decisions. With the risk of sounding sacrilegious, if you removed the God factor, is there anything else that might account for the decisions you're making about ministry and priorities?"

Truthfully, God sometimes gets too much credit and too much blame. We know that those in ministry often have personality characteristics that draw them to this profession: they tend to be caring and giving. Frequently they're pleasers who have difficulty saying no and have very high expectations of themselves. These characteristics alone would make it difficult to balance ministry and marriage. But for the men in this group, another theme emerged.

Each was driven to succeed in ministry at almost any cost. And this need to succeed was easily traced to their early-life experiences when their value as a person was erroneously connected to their ability to accomplish tasks. As boys, they desperately sought the praise of their fathers. And now as men, this need translated to their seeking the praise of others around them. They were driven to succeed, because it was success that made them feel worthy. This obsession to succeed was supported by the value system of the new millennium and their theology as well.

A Family Tradition

"My grandfather was a missionary in Africa. He would leave my grandmother and his five children alone for weeks or months at a time. I guess that's where my dad learned it was OK to sacrifice family in the name of ministry."

Sacrificing family in the name of ministry—Brett was describing a philosophy that defined his 15-year marriage and almost ruined the most important relationship in his life. After all, this type of behavior had been legitimized by culture: "No pain, no gain." It had been legitimized by his theology: "No sacrifice is too great to satisfy the call of God on your life." And it had been legitimized by example—a family tradition passed on from generation to generation. Then Brett decided to break the cycle.

"I don't want my children to grow up doing the things I've done—or even thinking that it's right," he said. "I don't want it for my son when he becomes a husband and father, or for my daughter when she becomes a wife and mother. They deserve better than that.

"I deserved better when I was a boy, but I think my dad was doing the best he knew to do. I've had my priorities messed up, and it's not hard to figure out where that came from. I know better now, and this is one tradition that's going to stop in my generation."

It's not easy to go against the grain, whether the grain happens to be the world or the things we hold a little more sacred, such as the views of the religious community and our own families. That's a truth that Brett learned the hard way. Still, we will either set our own priorities, or we'll find them set for us by others. And when they're set for us, the tendency is always for these to pull us farther away from the relationships that matter most. We may succeed in areas that others think we ought to, but at what cost? A marriage is a terrible thing to waste regardless of the success we may achieve in any other area of life.

Are the Good Things Getting You Down?

"We can't seem to fit everything in." A common complaint among clergy couples and a problem made doubly difficult when you consider that "everything" usually refers to good things. How do you prioritize your life in such a manner that everything can fit in—including time for your marriage? You can't. No matter what the world is selling as truth, whether it be (1) "You can get it done" or (2) "Don't worry about your marriage—it'll be all right as you pursue the sacred cow of success," they're nothing but lies. The truth is, if you're going to have the kind of marriage God intended for you, you're going to have to schedule your marriage as a top priority, you're going to have to let go of some things, and having an intimate relationship is going to cost you something.

When it comes to marriage, being in the world but not of the world will mean recognizing what's truth and what's not. Trying to fit everything in will only result in pulling you away from what matters most—your spouse. Remember: an intimate marriage does not occur by accident. It's the result of intent. If you don't prioritize your life, the world will do it for you. So schedule your priorities and grow your marriage God's way.

12

Donald Harvey

Just When We Figure Out the Answers, Someone Changes the Questions

S haron was exasperated with her life. She didn't want counseling—just a sounding board and someone to help her gain perspective about her situation. I was glad to listen when we met at a retreat for pastors and their wives.

As Sharon shared what was on her heart, what struck me most about her story was not that it was unusual, but that it seemed so familiar.

Sharon and Bill met in college and married shortly after graduation. Bill began his ministry, and they started their family. Now, 15 years and three children later, with Bill in his third pastorate, Sharon is asking, "Why can't we get back to the *us* in this marriage?" The marriage, the careers, and the increased stress that comes with three children all seemed typical. Interestingly, it was the commonness of her predicament that fascinated me.

"Life's got too many moving parts," she explained. "It was tough for Bill and me to adjust to three small children. But when my youngest finally got in school, I thought things would fall back into some sort of order. Before I knew it, though, we were dealing with the chaos of parenting teenagers. It seems that just when we figure out one phase of our life, life changes. We figure out the answers, and someone changes the questions."

Sharon talked about the challenges of living with a teenager and the changes in their homelife necessitated by those challenges. Never far from her mind was the knowledge that two more of their children were racing toward their teens also. Added into the mix were church folks who were oblivious to the fact that when Sharon's life changed at home, it also affected what she could and couldn't do at church.

"I guess some people forget what it's like to have children at home," she said. "It's as if I'm not supposed to change what I do at church, even though the needs of my children have changed. That's a little frustrating—but nothing I can't handle. I think they'll get used to me not being as available as I was.

"The real problem with all of these changes is what they end up meaning for Bill and me. It's hard enough for me to make the adjustments. But Bill is a man who doesn't deal well with change. He likes to find a rhythm and stay there. What bothers me most is that we as a couple are getting lost in the shuffle. We've been so busy keeping up with our children that we lost track of the relationship between the two of us. Having kids pushes the couple thing to the back burner. But now I feel we've been taken off the stove. I sense that we're disconnecting."

Sharon thought she was experiencing something unique. The truth is, it's quite common. Her feelings were important and quite valid, but what she described happens very frequently. Not every couple disconnects as she and Bill had, but every couple faces the same kinds of challenges. Sharon was describing the different stages of the marital life cycle. And though these phases were a new experience for her, they were not novel. They were predictable.

The Cycle of Married Life

In the chapter titled "We Can't Seem to Fit Everything In," I identified the challenges marriages face from the outside. In this chapter we'll look at the challenges from inside your relationship that occur merely by the passage of time. Marriages pass through predictable stages, and adjustments will need to be made during each stage for you and your spouse to continuing growing together.

Remember God's simple two-stage model for healthy marriages I referred to earlier? You *leave,* and then you *join*—and you'll spend the rest of your life developing an intimate relationship with your spouse. God's focus has always been on joining—whether preparing yourself to join by leaving your family of origin, or blending into one flesh with the one you love.

There will always be the challenge of maintaining the two of you as a couple in the midst of life's demands. However, as the phases of your marriage evolve, the types of challenges you face will vary greatly. The challenges to intimacy encountered by a couple just beginning their family are different from those encountered by a couple whose children are nearly grown.

Before we dissect the phases of marriage, let's look at a couple of principles to be aware of.

First, the stages of the marital life cycle are determined by your circumstances, not your age. For instance, you face family issues when your first child comes along, not because you suddenly turn 20, 30, or 40. Second, how well you meet and adjust to the challenges of any stage in your journey is influenced by how well you dealt with what preceded it. Doing what needs to be done before you have children prepares you for what comes when you do. Just like building a house, you work from the foundation up. If the foundation is wrong, you can expect to have problems when you start putting up the walls. With this in mind, let's look at the predictable steps of your marital journey, concentrating on ministry couples.

The Independents

You're probably well beyond the single young adult stage, but we'll start there for the sake of thoroughness. After all, leaving home is the first stage of the marital life cycle. And there's another reason for starting here, because—remember the second principle—how well you deal with a particular stage is influenced by how well you dealt with what preceded it. That means that this earliest stage may have affected what's happening in your marriage today. Troy and Lucy are a prime example.

Troy and Lucy came for counseling because their relationship was growing more and more tense. This contradicted the image they were trying to present to their congregation, that of a deeply loving couple. Each had a long list of superficial complaints early on, but the real stuff surfaced during the fourth counseling session. Troy began the session with a complaint directed at Lucy: "You've always valued your mother's opinion over mine." I expected Lucy to quickly deny Troy's accusation, since that was their usual pattern of interaction. However, Lucy did just the opposite. "The Bible says a *man* will leave *his* father and mother—it says nothing about the woman doing that!" I thought she was trying to be funny. I was wrong. Lucy believed she was justified in failing to make the break from her family. As it turned out, Troy hadn't made that break either. From a developmental perspective, their failure to reach that early goal was interfering with their success in their present phase.

I refer to single young adults as *independents,* because the object of this stage of life is to separate from family and become freestanding adults, self-reliant and independent. One of the hallmarks of the successful completion of this phase of life is the ability to make independent decisions. Do the decisions you make reflect what you think or more what your parents and friends think? Lucy's decisions were overly influenced by her mother's opinions. She had not yet achieved independence. A friend of mine once commented that a healthy marriage consists of two whole people; and someone who has not left home is not whole.

The Lovers

Lovers are newly married couples. You plunge into this stage when you say, "I do," and it lasts until the arrival of your first child. The goal of this stage is for the two of you to firmly establish your relationship. You may be thinking that you were in this relationship for quite some time before the wedding, and that's true. But the level of commitment changed with your wedding vows. Your relationship became more intense. It's during this time of bonding that you really get to know each other and begin to adjust to your life together.

The keys to success during this step in your marital journey are *boundaries* and *prioritization.* You begin to establish a boundary around your relationship, clearly defining yourselves as a couple. You'll accomplish this as you prioritize each other above other people and activities. The integrity of your marriage may be challenged in several ways. Perhaps you will allow a parent to exert more influence over decisions than your spouse. Friends and activities may take precedence over time. You may invest heavily in a career at the expense of the relationship. These are examples of *lovers' breakdown*—a challenging of boundaries and prioritization. A common complaint I hear from couples experiencing lovers' breakdown is "I don't feel that I count in this marriage."

Though each of these examples can occur in ministry marriages, the potential for becoming overinvolved in career endeavors especially plagues clergy couples. With most of the parsonage couples I've counseled, the temptation to prioritize ministry over marriage has occurred very early in the marriage. Sometimes marriages just don't get off on the right foot.

The Harried

The most demanding stage in the marital journey begins when the babies come along. You may be so harried you don't even know what you're doing—you only know you're doing a lot of it! Nothing changes your home more than the demands of an infant. No more sleeping in. No more spontaneous trips, not even to the grocery store, much less out of town. Everything you do now requires planning and the use of a U-Haul for the extra gear. Kiss romance good-bye, and say hello to the zombie who's taken over your spouse's body. You have entered the "harried zone."

So what's the goal for your marriage at this stage? Simply this: making the leap from a couple to a family, from the two of you to the three of you—and not losing the marriage.

Kim sought counseling already realizing that she and Howard had not done well with this goal. "I'm vulnerable right now, and I know it," she said. "I know what's right and wrong—I'm a pastor's wife. My head says I'll always do the right thing. But there's no one tempting me right now, and to be honest, I have to admit I really don't know what I'd do if someone else suddenly came into my life."

Kim described her marriage as fine until children came along, but I question whether she and Howard had really gotten off on the right foot in the first place. It sounded to me as if church got more than the lion's share of their time even back then. But I couldn't argue with Kim's assessment of what happened after their daughter came along: "Things got more and more hectic. It was all I could do to keep up with Jamie—feedings, naps, baths—much less the house. There were times when I just let everything else go. Howard wasn't much help in the early months, and he didn't get any better as Jamie got older. Sometimes I just wanted to hear an adult voice, but he was always gone. The battle lines were drawn; he threw himself into the ministry, and I threw myself into parenting. We both got into the marriage survival mode. We lost *us,* and I don't know how to get that back."

This is a time when we have to work hard at carving out time for our marriage. The temptation is to just collapse at home and attempt to relax. But to recharge your emotional batteries, you have to *relate*. Staying connected requires intent and planning, and neither Kim nor Howard had grasped this. They had missed the big picture of *joining*, and thus they emotionally disconnected. Unless they got balance back in their marriage, they would experience continuing difficulties as they faced the predictable demands for change that would come their way by the mere passage of time.

The Releasers

Just when you think you've got parenting down, your kids enter adolescence—the next stage of the marital life cycle—and you're forced to change again. After all, you don't parent a 15-year-old adolescent the same way you parent a 5-year-old child—though some will try. This is when parents must begin to release their kids and start the process of letting go.

During this stage, kids receive increasingly more freedom and the corresponding responsibilities while parents become increasingly more flexible and less controlling. Sounds easy enough. It's not. The transition of power associated with parenting an adolescent is more analogous to traveling over a mountain road inundated with potholes and ruts than traveling a smooth superhighway. Basically, from the teen's perspective, you're too slow in releasing the reins. And from your perspective, he or she wants too much too soon. So the push-pull begins. If the harried couple was worn out from the physical demands of parenting, the *releasers* are weary from the sheer emotional strain. This is a time that tries the patience of most parents, when survival is an admirable goal. "Let's just get through this!" But what does this mean for you as a couple?

This is the stage that Sharon and Bill were in—the couple mentioned at the beginning of our chapter. They had three children, and the oldest had just entered adolescence. Sharon saw her situation as unique—but, in fact, it was predictable. Remember Sharon's concern: "The rules have changed. Bill and I have moved from the back burner to completely off the stove. I feel that we're disconnecting." They probably were. I don't think they had weathered the previous stage too well—they had already begun to get lost in the shuffle with young children. But the changes required for dealing with adolescents, the flexing of the rules dictated by living with teens, now seemed to consume what little bit of energy they had been directing toward their marriage. Sharon was right to be concerned. They were beginning to flounder.

This change in the rules was just another stressor on life's highway, something else to pull Sharon and Bill farther away from where they needed to be and what they needed to be doing for their marriage. Certainly, this was a time when they as parents needed to be in consensus—a difficult task to achieve if they were disconnected emotionally. But disconnecting could have even graver consequences for their marriage. Marriages that drift apart during this stage are sometimes impossible to reconnect. An empty marriage contradicts God's design, and it is extremely vulnerable.

The Launchers

Launching is good. You love your children, but you raise them to leave. That's the natural order of things. You become a *launcher* when your first child leaves home for college, a career, or marriage. This stage demands that you really start the process of letting go, and it's a *process*. It's not accomplished in one giant step, and launching has a lot of implications for your marriage. It allows for some new experiences, but it also allows for the resumption of some old standbys. It's at this time in the marriage that you begin to redefine your relationship. You may begin to ask yourself what your relationship will look like when it's just the two of you again.

Some things will get easier. There will be more room for spontaneity. There will be more time to do things together. Keeping up the house will take less time, making it easier to get away together. But all of this is predicated on the fact that you still *want to*. Launching is good, but it seems to be better for some than it is for others. This is noted by the startling divorce statistics. Twenty percent of divorces occur during this stage of marriage—when things ought to be getting easier.

Launching is predictably better for couples who have managed to establish the couple connection early on and then maintain it when the demands of kids are at their highest. The couples understand the big picture and continue to join. It's not so good for everyone else—the wife and mother who threw herself into her children, and the husband who threw himself into his ministry. Now what are they to do? It may be that the children were all they really talked about for the last several years. Now that they're gone or leaving, there's nothing to say to each other. At least, that's how one couple expressed it: "I got up one morning and asked myself, 'What do we have?' The answer was a big, fat zero. We got our kids raised, and I praise God for that. But who is this man sitting across from me? I don't know him. I think I used to—but not anymore. We need to be reintroduced."

The rules are changing again, and that means you have to change too. That may not feel comfortable, but this is also a time with so much potential for your relationship. It's easier to focus on the joining—whether you're just continuing what you've been doing all along or rediscovering something that you somehow misplaced. It's never too late to get back into God's plan.

The Recliners

During the last stage of the marital life cycle, retirement, you become a *recliner*. Your adjustments tend to center around space and time. This was noted on a plaque I saw recently that offered the following definition for retirement: "Twice the husband and half the money." Living with half the money (a fixed income) gets a lot of press. But it's surviving the "twice the husband" (space and time issues) that motivates couples to contact the counselor. When John and Susan came to my office, they described their situation this way:

John—I've got good news and bad news. The good news is that I've got more time to spend with Susan. The bad news is that I've got more time to spend with Susan.

Susan—I married him for better or for worse—not for lunch.

It's a little more complicated than simply boiling it down to space and time. For instance, there are some individual concerns. I think women, who tend to have a more instrumental role in child rearing, have more difficulty with the *launching* stage than their husbands. Men, with a large part of their ego attached to their careers, have a more difficult time with retirement. Personal difficulties like these can contribute to relational difficulties. But as John and Susan articulated, the big adjustment for *recliners* is how to manage the extra time they now find on their hands.

The formula for healthy relationships still holds: his, hers, and theirs. The amount of time to devote to each may have changed with this new status in life, but some degree of balance must be maintained. Husbands and wives don't have to spend every waking moment together. In fact, it's better if they don't. It's OK for each to have hobbies and interests that do not include the other. And it's OK for them to have friends and support circles that aren't identical. And it's OK to acknowledge that you need a little space—a little private time when your spouse won't be underfoot. The goal is balance. Too much of a good thing—or a good person—is, well, too much.

If the golden years are golden, it probably didn't happen by accident. As with all the other stages, making adjustments for time and space is more easily accomplished by those who have done well with the challenges of the preceding stages. Those who have maintained a connection throughout their marriage and even reshaped it during the launching phase will be better off than those who have not kept the big picture in focus. Being a *recliner* can be a time of unequaled richness. In a marriage that's been built on mutuality, in which each spouse is sensitive to the needs of the other, in which sacrifices have been willingly made in the other's best interest, and in which no other person or thing has claimed higher priority—the blessings of faithfulness will be found.

It's Easy to Drift

Drifting is the gradual and subtle emotional disconnection that takes place in a marriage when spouses become more concerned with *function* than *relationship*. Couples don't intend to drift, but because life is so demanding, it sometimes just naturally occurs. It's easy to drift—and one of the reasons is the constant change inherent in family life.

Successfully predicting the need for adjustment doesn't mean we'll successfully adjust. But maybe with a little help in knowing what to expect, we can intend to stay connected. Drifting happens easily, but it's not a given. You can have an intimate marriage—even with children. You just have to plan for it. Like the old adage points out—if things aren't going according to plan, maybe there never was a plan. God's big picture is for intimate relationships—and it's achievable. Plan, commit, and work for it.

13

Gene Williams

The Great Myth

Y es, there really is a great myth circulating in Christendom. Simply stated, it's "If I commit everything to the ministry, to building God's kingdom, God will take care of my family. He watches out for His own. I'm excused from my responsibility as a husband and father as long as I'm engrossed in His work."

Of course, this just isn't true. Yet many ministerial families have fallen for it.

As I move across the country, I encounter preacher's kids who feel abandoned by their parents, especially their father. As a result they resent the church and, in many instances, have rebelled against God.

Sue was the granddaughter of a wonderful pastor whose leadership helped establish one of the great churches of his denomination. Later, he was a major force in salvaging one of their church's largest educational institutions. Along the way he instilled a love for God and ministry in the hearts of his sons, one of whom was called into the ministry. This son became a brilliant pastor and expositor of the gospel. He led churches through major building programs and erected great buildings across the country. Without a doubt, he was seen as a great man of God. The church proclaimed him a great success. And from the church's point of view, he was.

But he was a victim of "the great myth." He virtually ignored his family. When his wife couldn't take the neglect any longer, she took her daughters and left.

A Tragedy of Errors

As a result of this divorce, Sue and her sister grew up without the benefit of a caring father in their lives. He was so busy preparing great messages and building beautiful buildings that he had no time to help build the lives of his two innocent daughters. He thought that because he was actively advancing the Kingdom, surely God would take care of his family.

Sue did well for a while. She married a bright young ministerial student and helped him gain an excellent education. They had three children, and he made great strides in ministry. Then things began to fall apart. Her pastor-husband began to follow the pattern of her absentee father. True, he was preparing great messages and leading a vibrant congregation in building a beautiful place of worship. These were very good things. But to him the Kingdom was more important than anything else. He, like Sue's father, forgot that Jesus wanted him to express God's love for everyone—including his family.

Let me say it as strongly as possible: There's no contradiction in being a faithful minister and a faithful husband and father. Ministry begins at home, and every minister's primary mission field is his home address. It's not *either* ministry *or* family. It must be *both* ministry *and* family.

As a result of two ministers who bought into the myth, her father and then her husband, Sue left it all. She divorced her husband. Ultimately she lost her children. In a few years, feeling abandoned by those who should have cared for her, she began to make herself available to the many men who paid attention to her. In order to live with her aching conscience, she began to drink and soon became an alcoholic. Only she can be held accountable for what her life became. However, one has to wonder how different things might have been if her husband and father hadn't bought into "the great myth."

No Contradictions

Sue and I had been friends for many years when her late-night call came from halfway across the country. She needed to talk with someone who cared and would listen. Bettye and I soon realized she was drunk, and while Sue was responsible for the sin she had allowed to overtake her life, our hearts were broken by the mess from the fallout of "the great myth."

Unfortunately, many people exist only on the crumbs left behind on the service table of their ministry spouse. I've known wives who would think they were in heaven if their husband gave them some serious time.

I have a young friend in the ministry who appears to have biblically prioritized his life, even though his ministry requires extensive traveling. He has taken charge of his schedule so that he's at home when his kids are out of school. I asked him how he did it, and he replied, "I work hard when I'm away. Then I schedule a lot of early and late flights so I can get home quickly to be there for the maximum amount of time." He added, "I have seen too many of my contemporaries lose their families. I'm not going to let that happen." His family is living proof that his plan is working. His wife is happy, and their children love the church.

If You're Too Busy—You're Too Busy!

I know what it means to be busy. In the last 26 years of my ministry I pastored a church with nearly 2,000 members. At the same time I served on the boards of two colleges, the District Advisory Board of my denomination, and was president of the 300-church pastors' alliance for my city. In addition to preaching at least four times a week and teaching a large Sunday School class, I had several weddings and funerals every month. I know something about being busy.

My son Pat is a high school football coach, athletic director, and history teacher. These duties could translate to long hours away from his wife and sons. This isn't ministry in the strict sense, but there are some parallels worth considering.

Pat is in the establishing years of his career, and that means he must work harder than ever. He dearly loves his family, so I was not surprised when he called to say, "Pray for me, Dad. I'm going to have to make some adjustments in my job. I'm away from the family too much." Pat is not looking to leave coaching and teaching, but to relinquish the athletic director's position. Since it's primarily an administrative position, it's very time-consuming. In fact, the job keeps him away from his sons—the kids he is *most* called to influence.

Pat's work as a teacher and head coach not only is his dream job but also is what God called him to do. Once he was spiritually established himself, God called him to return to school and be trained to be a strong spiritual example for high school students. The Lord has blessed his efforts and has opened many doors for him.

So why is he concerned about his family? If he believed "the great myth," there would be no need to worry about the amount of time he's spending with his family. He could just pour himself into the assignment God has given him, and God would look out for his family. But he knows better than that. He will not abandon his family to pursue his career—even if it's God's calling on his life. So Pat is in God-directed pursuit of an arrangement that will enable him to be successful in the Lord's career plan for his life and also be the husband and father He desires him to be. Pat is going to adjust his schedule in order to be available to his family.

A Great Example

My good friend Tom pastors a thriving church of over 1,500. He recently led his congregation through a major building program and is involved in many areas of responsibility in our city. So how does he balance the responsibilities of pastor, husband, and father?

For one thing, Tom never—I mean never—misses his children's school activities. His son plays high school basketball, and Tom is committed to attending every game regardless of the distance involved. That's step one.

Tom took his son to the mountains of Colorado for a week last summer, and the two of them spent the entire time camping, laughing, riding dirt bikes, and doing fun things that teenage sons and fathers love to do. They took time to talk and pray together. They even went to Denver to a baseball game. Tom's son will surely remember that week forever. And he'll likely never feel resentment toward the demands of his father's pastorate.

Tom has a young daughter in need of her father's attention too. So the two of them flew to a major city for shopping, a trip to an amusement park, long talks, and prayer time. He treated her to a major league ball game as well. I'm sure Tom's daughter is confident and secure in her father's love.

Though Tom's schedule didn't really allow time for these important activities, he was wise enough to *make* the time. His church didn't suffer while he enveloped his children in love. He and his wife have a warm, loving relationship, and it pleases her when Tom spends time with their children.

Establishing Boundaries

When my children were small, I pastored a growing church. There were almost constant activities that I was expected to attend, and I was responsible for denominational youth activities for nearly 10,000 teenagers in the state of Florida. I was meeting myself coming and going, but I was determined to be all things to all people.

One evening I was gobbling down my supper when my nine-year-old son stopped me in my tracks. "You're not a very good daddy," he said. His words pierced my heart like a knife. He continued: "You never take time for us."

Driving home from my meeting later that night, I took the pain of that accusation to the Lord. He took my son's side.

"When are the kids out of school?"

"On Saturdays, Lord."

"So what's more important—golf with your buddies, or your kids?"

On Sunday morning I announced to my congregation that Saturday would be my day off. I would be available only for emergencies. My people supported me in that decision. As a matter of fact, it became a good model for other fathers in my church.

From then on, Saturday was my day for the family. We faced some exceptions when a church member became critically ill or died—shepherds must be available when they're truly needed. But God blessed my decision, and my church respected my commitment to my family.

I learned a lot about boundaries during my time at that church. I'm so thankful that He opened my eyes to the great myth.

The Rewards of Faithfulness

You know, I've never received the recognition and adoration that Sue's father and husband did. My family sometimes faced long struggles and difficult moments, but my children never felt I had abandoned them. And they all five serve the Lord today.

Of course, there are exceptions to every rule. Parents who do everything right sometimes have wayward children anyway. These parents were available to their children, spent time with them, prayed with them and for them, and were great examples. Still, these children became prodigals. It's helpful, though, if you can look yourself in the face and know you've been faithful. That knowledge carried me through a 10-year period of rebellion by one of my children. And I'm sure there have been ministerial spouses who have plunged into the abyss of sin in spite of having loving, attentive, Christlike husbands. Just hold yourself accountable for your faithfulness to your family.

So how do you spend *your* Saturdays? Are your kids still young? How about going home for lunch and hanging around for naptime? Establish your priorities.

My son Steve would be the first to tell you that after our little talk at dinner, I became a good daddy. And I'm proud to say he's a good daddy too.

A Fertile Field

I could name them, but I won't. Their names and faces will come to your mind—the "great" evangelists and spiritual leaders who have learned the hard lessons of "the great myth."

Their biographies bemoan the fact that they were absentee fathers. While they were winning the world—a noble calling—their wives were left alone to raise their children. In many cases, the mother alone was no match for the lure of the non-Christian world. Father was harvesting for God, but no one was working the field at home. Without a doubt, God's call is worthy of our best effort and highest possible involvement. But we dare not forget the mission field at our home address. He has given you the task of loving your children into the Kingdom. Don't let Him down.

14

Donald Harvey

It Starts with the Heart

J an and I both realized that my life was out of control. We talked about it several times, and we neither liked it nor denied it. The hard part was figuring out what to do about it. I wasn't doing anything bad. In fact, the opposite was true. I was doing too many good things. I was drowning in the sea of Christendom. I was a university professor teaching in and administering a graduate program in marriage and family therapy. I was a therapist counseling couples and supervising the activities of other therapists. I was a sought-after speaker at conferences and training seminars. I had the desire to write—a passion that was being neglected—and I was a churchman conducting retreats. I was the victim of good things.

I began to sense that I wasn't doing anything well. I was doing OK—but not well. The difference in doing things OK and doing things well was beginning to frustrate me. And I was neglecting things I really wanted to do. I was responding to the call of the urgent. The most significant discovery, though, was when I realized I was doing more and more and enjoying it less and less. Yes, things were certainly out of control.

About this time, Jan and I were invited to Colorado to look at becoming involved in yet another ministry opportunity. Ironically, it was a ministry to clergy couples in crisis. We didn't know what God had in mind for us in Colorado, and I don't know that either of us really thought it would lead to our actually becoming part of the ministry. But we both felt we were definitely supposed to go. So we accepted the invitation and intended to be open to God's leading. We also took this opportunity to reassess our lives. We were both ready for something to change.

Choices, Choices, Choices

As we talked in Colorado, we recognized that there were some things over which we had little control. I could leave the university where I was teaching, and that would significantly reduce some of the demands on my life. But neither of us saw that as a real solution. God had led us there, and if He led us away, we would obediently follow another call. But He didn't appear to be doing that. So if we remained at the university, there were some things that just went with the territory and couldn't be altered. I also realized that even in a university environment there were some things over which I did have influence. I could exert more control over my life on campus—but would I? I could adapt my schedule, realign responsibilities, let some things go, reassess future commitments, learn when to say no. Yes, there were things I *could* do. But would I really follow through on the necessary changes?

As Jan and I talked, I had to admit that if I were honest with myself, I could easily reconstruct the chaos no matter where I was or what I was doing. And though we were both creative people—planning had never been a difficult thing for us to do—we both realized that this problem would not be solved by our simply developing a new plan and merely figuring out a better way to do things. Something deeper was required.

First Things First

I don't believe the things in life that create the most difficulty lose their grip on us because they suddenly become easier. I think we just finally become resolute. And that's the message we get from Scripture.

Luke is my favorite Gospel writer. I like his tendency to be precise, his attention to detail. We seem to see more of this in Luke's Gospel than we do in those of his cohorts.

This difference in writing style is noted in the recording of Jesus' pivotal turn toward Jerusalem. In a real sense, Jesus' entire ministry was a journey to Jerusalem. He occasionally spoke of it as "destination" and "destiny." In those early times of His ministry, He was content to travel through the Galilean and Judean countryside ministering to people and investing in the lives of the disciples.

Then things changed. The preparation period had ended. It was time to move toward His destiny—the reason He came to be the

God-Man. It was time to go to Jerusalem. This was a monumental time in His ministry and greatly significant for the future of humanity. How did the Gospel writers record this pivotal event? Mathew records the turn toward Jerusalem like this:

Jesus was going up to Jerusalem.

—Matt. 20:17

Mark states it nearly as simply:

They were on their way up to Jerusalem, with Jesus leading the way.

—Mark 10:32

Both Gospel writers go on to say that Jesus took the disciples aside and explained the events that would take place in Jerusalem —the arrest, the condemnation, the death, and the Resurrection. But no attention is given to the significance of changing the focus of Jesus' ministry. It's as if they were all on a guided tour, and the next stop happened to be Jerusalem. At least, no attention is given to it other than by Luke.

To Luke, more than simple events were taking place, and he wanted to make sure we understood the significance of what had occurred. Luke captured the essence of the turn toward Jerusalem when he stated,

As the time approached for him to be taken up to heaven, Jesus resolutely set out for Jerusalem.

—Luke 9:51

Why did Jesus *resolutely set out* for Jerusalem? Why a resolute turn? Jesus turned resolutely because He knew what lay ahead. He knew the betrayal. He knew the mocking. He knew the disappointment, the abandonment, the aloneness. And He knew the pain. He knew what was to come. But it was time, so He resolutely set His face toward Jerusalem.

Jesus was concerned that His disciples understand His resolve. He gave three examples, all recorded by Luke, illustrating precisely what being resolute is and precisely what it is not.

As they were walking along the road, a man said to him, "I will follow you wherever you go."

Jesus replied, "Foxes have holes and birds of the air have nests, but the Son of Man has no place to lay his head."

He said to another man, "Follow me." But the man replied, "Lord, first let me go and bury my father."

Jesus said to him, "Let the dead bury their own dead, but you go and proclaim the kingdom of God."

Still another said, "I will follow you, Lord; but first let me go back and say good-by to my family."

Jesus replied, "No one who puts his hand to the plow and looks back is fit for service in the kingdom of God."

—Luke 9:57-62

The first illustration is of a man they met along the road who said, "I will follow you wherever you go." At first, we may find Jesus' response puzzling. What do foxes and birds have to do with it? But Jesus' focus was on being resolute, on what goes into our making decisions. His decision to turn toward Jerusalem was not made flippantly. He *knew* what was going to take place. He understood the cost. And with this knowledge, He chose to move toward His destiny. His decision flowed from His *awareness*, not from ignorance. He wanted the man on the road to do the same. It's as if He were saying, "Don't give me an easy, hasty, automatic response. These are the facts. Be sure. Evaluate, count the costs, look at the situation, and calculate. And with full forethought, make your decision. Don't make it flippantly, because much will be required of you. Are you sure you're ready?"

This example is followed by two "yes, but" illustrations. Two men are asked separately to follow Jesus. Both are willing but have pressing business that first requires attention. Jesus' response in both of these situations clarifies what being resolute is not. To the first He said, "Let the dead bury their own dead." And to the other He said, "No one who puts his hand to the plow and looks back is fit for service in the kingdom of God."

Following Jesus requires a resolute decision, not a flippant one or one based on ignorance. It's a well-informed and well-thought-out commitment. Neither can it be one with divided loyalties, as respectable as these other responsibilities may be. *Resolute* means being ready to follow, regardless.

What does all of this have to do with ministry marriages? If you're going to have the kind of marriage that God designed, you have to "go to Jerusalem." You have to *choose* to prioritize your marriage—not flippantly, not halfheartedly, but resolutely. If being a therapist has taught me anything, it's this: *Things change not because they become easy, but because we become resolute.* Whether it's personal problems or dissatisfaction in your marriage, if you're content to wait until things get easy, the likelihood of any significant change is doubtful. Things change because you honestly face the issues and assume responsibility for what you find. You take control of your life.

Going Forward Resolutely

Jan and I returned from Colorado with resolve. We were determined to see changes in our lives. Gradually I began to regain control. Having first made the decision to change, I began envisioning what that might look like. I created a plan. And then, even more gradually, I began to implement the plan. Change didn't come in a day. It seldom does. True change is more a *process* than an event. But my decision to regain control of my life was an event. I remember when and where I made the decision. And the process just naturally followed. That's the order of things.

Taking control of your marriage will come in a similar fashion. It won't come because you create a great plan. And it won't come instantaneously. It will take time. But one thing is for sure—it won't occur at all unless you first make a decision to do so. There must be a change of heart—we call this commitment—before any plan can work. But with the resolve to change, almost anything can be accomplished. Even getting your marriage back.

Give Me a Formula!

Thinking in terms of resolve and commitment is becoming less and less common in the new millennium. That's because neither is simple nor easy. And one of the characteristics of new millennium thinking is that we want it simple and easy. We're used to frozen dinners and fast food. We want solutions to our problems served up the same way. We want pat answers requiring little thought. We want canned approaches. You know how it works—a five-step program guaranteed to bring a quick solution, not something that takes into account that we have been uniquely created. We want the warm fuzzies and niceties. Forget "awkward," reject "uncomfortable," deny "difficult." We even want our theology in a formula—"if you just do this, everything will work out fine." Give me prosperity. Don't talk about pain.

The older I get, the more I dislike lists. I think they lull us into a false sense of security, just like other cookie-cutter formulas that over-simplify complex situations. "If I just do this or that, then everything will work out." Life's not like that. And marriage definitely doesn't work that way. I can't give you a formula for change. You'll have to create your own plan. But I *will* tell you this: *If things are going to change at all in your marriage, it will happen because you experience a change of heart.* If it doesn't start with the heart, it won't last.

Your heart changes when you finally recognize the truth, when you get a glimpse of what marital health is all about. Your heart changes when you compare what ought to be going on in your marriage with what is actually taking place and decide that you don't like the difference between the two. And your heart changes when you decide you're ready to act instead of react—regardless of the cost. You're going to do something to change your life. When your heart changes, your marriage changes. Without a heart change, behavioral changes will be short-lived. You can have a better marriage. But you first have to decide that you want it. There's definitely an order to things, and it starts with the heart.

15

Donald Harvey

Our Unique Interferences: Sometimes Things Just Aren't So Simple

I traveled to Indonesia several years ago to counsel with missionaries serving there. It was my first international trip, and for that reason alone, I expected it to be a special experience. Passports, visas, shots, customs officials, 14 time zones, traveling on airlines with names I couldn't pronounce—all were new to me.

I've always viewed new experiences as learning opportunities. Thinking I might pick up some tips on how to make my travels easier, I paid particular attention to other passengers on the flight. It was easy to tell the seasoned veterans from the first timers. For example, once we were airborne for the 12-hour flight, the seasoned travelers immediately got up from their assigned seats and began seeking out better accommodations. There was no announcement over the intercom. No bell was sounded. Nothing happened to suggest that anything had changed. They just got up and moved. They knew the rules: if you can find several vacant seats together in a row, voilà—you have a bed. I didn't know the rules. I spent 12 hours trying to sleep in an upright position without falling over onto the person next to me. I'm a quick learner, though—I had a bed on the return flight!

I also learned a few things about counseling in an intense environment. In Nashville I see couples for an hour or so on a weekly basis. Occasionally we meet for a little longer than an hour. And every now and then we'll wait a week or two between sessions.

That's about it for big changes in my routine. Things are far different in the field. I didn't have several months to work with these missionary couples—I had only two weeks. So I had to adapt. I ended up intensifying the therapy process by increasing the time spent in session to at least two hours and decreasing the amount of time between sessions by meeting on a daily or every-other-day basis.

Aha!

I believe these missionary couples benefited from this experience, as I prayed they would. But I benefited too. I learned some new things about God—particularly the way He reaches out to His people. And I learned some things about myself and my ability to adapt to new and challenging situations. I also learned some things about others, especially in regard to their problems.

I was peering "through a glass, darkly" (1 Cor. 13:12, KJV) before going to Indonesia. I somehow saw missionaries as being different from the rest of us. I assumed that any marital problems I found would be related to the unique characteristics of their calling, that somehow, being missionaries on a foreign field had placed a hardship on these couples and that the stress *on* the marriage had caused stress *in* the marriage. I was wrong. That was a simple explanation for a complex problem. No doubt, these couples were experiencing pressures. What surprised me, though, was finding that their problems had nothing to do with geography.

Troubled marriages are a lot like looking at a china cup with a hairline crack. The crack goes unnoticed while the cup is sitting on the table. When you hold the cup up to the light, however, the crack becomes visible. The light didn't cause the crack—it only illuminates it. When couples experience difficulties in their relationship, stress is seldom the culprit. Stress doesn't create a problem between spouses—it simply reveals what's already present in the relationship.

As we spent intensive hours together, we began to identify hairline cracks in these marriages. Some had been there for quite a while. In fact, some were even older than the marriages themselves; they had been brought into the relationship by one or both spouses. But in every instance, these marital cracks were greater than either *calling* or *context*. Just like the luggage that had been painstakingly hauled around from one airport to another during their trek to Indonesia, their problems had also been brought with them.

Oh, for the Simple Life!

How we long for the simple things in life! Simple problems, simple solutions, pat answers. We want everything converted to quick formulas for success. We even have something called "brief therapy" so we can conserve time and money.

When I gave up my simple ideas about the missionaries and realized that geography wasn't the issue and that the problems they were having could just as easily occur if they had never left the States, I began to see what was really happening in these marriages. Suddenly I was on familiar territory. Communication issues, conflict over marital roles, resentments, dissatisfaction with the level of intimacy in their relationships, control issues—I had seen it all before. But before, it had been in the lives of businessmen, homemakers, and teachers.

I could have stuck with my simple perception that their problems were the result of calling or context. But I would have missed the real problems, and I probably would have been of no help to them. Sometimes the things that cause problems and what it takes to solve them just aren't simple.

I would like to think I had made some great, new discovery—but I didn't. At best, it was only a *re*discovery. Louis McBurney found that things aren't always as simple as they appeared several years earlier. He made the discovery while counseling with people in ministry:

> I have found that among the ministers whom I have counseled, vocational or theological issues have been relatively infrequent as primary causes for their problems. Instead, most have come with basic personality difficulties related to early-life experiences that were *brought along into* the ministry. It is true, however, that the particular stresses of the calling have in some instances *intensified* a conflict which otherwise might have remained undisturbed (*Every Pastor Needs a Pastor* [Marble, Colo.: Marble Retreat, 1977], 92, emphasis added).

In the early 1970s Dr. McBurney and his wife, Melissa, founded Marble Retreat, an intensive treatment ministry for clergy in crisis. Caring for hurting pastors and wives was a calling that God placed on their hearts as they recognized the unique pressures experienced by men and women in ministry. They also recognized that, much like the missionary couples in Indonesia, the problems that finally brought them to the point of crisis had more to do with *them* than it did with their position.

When I Was a Child . . .

Ron was in the third year of his first pastorate and had been married to Shelly five years when they first came to see me. As is sometimes the case, they didn't completely agree on why they were coming to counseling or what was happening in their marriage. Shelly complained that she was the only one working on the relationship, that Ron was overinvolved in the ministry and underinvolved in their marriage. "I believe that if I stopped initiating contact with Ron, we'd completely disconnect." Ron vehemently disagreed. When I asked Ron to tell his side of things and to specifically note the things he was doing to invest in his marriage, the conversation somewhat dried up. He couldn't come up with anything tangible to support his view.

There was one thing they agreed upon completely: "We can't seem to communicate." What they meant was that they could never get resolution of any kind. They argued incessantly. It didn't matter how big or little the issue—it was beyond their ability to get any kind of consensus.

> *Ron*—We can't communicate. Whenever we try to deal with a problem, it never ends well. We never get resolution. We just end up getting mad at each other and walking away. We both know it shouldn't be this way. We're Christians, and it ought to be better than this. But we just can't get it fixed.
>
> We need you to teach us a better way to communicate. You know, how to fight fair and all that other stuff. Maybe you could give us a book to read or something. We definitely need to learn some new skills.

Ron seemed to know already what the problem was and had a solution in mind, which made me wonder why he and Shelly thought they needed me. It is somewhat typical, though, for clients to see their problems as simple, and in their eyes the solutions will be just as simple.

I didn't try to intervene in their communication problem during that first session. I didn't know them well enough to form an accurate opinion about what was really going on, and they didn't know me well enough to let me try to change them. So I just watched and waited for a session or two as I gathered information about their backgrounds. I wanted to know what each had brought to the marriage from their own families and exactly how this may have affected what they had developed within the relationship.

Sure enough, they didn't communicate very well. But there was a pattern to the way they did it. Shelly always initiated the conversation. But she appeared to be forced into that role by Ron. Remember how she was afraid that if she stopped initiating contact that they would just disconnect? It appeared that this was a legitimate concern. Ron played a passive role. He would not initiate. But though he would not initiate, he definitely would respond. And his response was always in *opposition* to whatever Shelly had just stated. If she said it was daylight outside, Ron would find some way to disagree with her position.

So Ron and Shelly were partially correct. They did have a communication problem. But it wasn't as simple as they thought. It wasn't that they didn't know how to communicate; at some level, they were choosing not to communicate. A book on healthy communication wasn't going to change anything. Although that might work for other couples, it wasn't going to do anything for Ron and Shelly. Their problem was complex, and there would be no simple solution. Change was going to require more than a few new skills.

When people are stuck in patterns that don't allow them to do the things they know they should do, you have to wonder why. What's really going on here? The answers were buried in what each had brought into the marriage, especially Ron. Ron described his family as ideal. A closer look challenged his assessment. True, he was raised in a stable and caring environment. But it was dominated by women. His mother exercised the power in the home, which operated on "If mama ain't happy, ain't nobody happy." Ron was the youngest child, and the next two oldest siblings were girls. These sisters were very protective and carefully watched out for their little brother. This arrangement worked fine in his younger years, but as Ron grew older he began to feel smothered.

Encircled by powerful women, and feeling helpless to elicit change, Ron resorted to passive resistance. He would never stand up and fight, but he could drag his feet with the best of them.

Shelly was not a controlling woman. She wasn't out to smother Ron. She didn't want to be his mother or his sister—just his wife. But

Ron couldn't tell the difference, because he had not yet *put off child-ish things*. He had learned to survive at home and gain some sense of self by resisting the women in his life. And now, though no longer a child, Ron continued to replicate this dynamic in his adult relationships. What was going on between him and Shelly had nothing to do with their not knowing how to communicate. It wasn't about that. It was much deeper than that—at his very core. For Ron it was about survival. Though not a strongly conscious thought, Ron felt he would completely lose himself if he were to give in on anything.

Change did not come easily for Ron and Shelly. But it did come. And what precipitated the change was when Ron honestly began to see the problem. He had to give up his simple solutions, and he had to stop blaming Shelly for his problems. He began to look deeply within himself.

When Things Get Stuck, Ask Why and Seek Help

Our goal in previous chapters was to identify the unique challenges of pastoral ministry for both the pastor and the spouse. We've discussed God's design for marriage and examined the kinds of things that go on in healthy and growing relationships—boundaries, prioritization, emotional investment, and so on. We've identified the ways you can sense ministry pressure from within your relationship and from outside sources. And we've identified the challenges of prioritizing. With this in mind, you can now contrast what's happening in your marriage with what should be happening.

Figuring out what you should do is a start—but it's only a start. And sometimes it's the easiest piece of the puzzle. A colleague once told me his view of counseling. He observed that the real art of therapy is not in figuring out what people ought to do—it's in getting them to do it. I think he's right. And that really ties into the point of this chapter. *Things aren't always as simple as they appear, and change isn't always as easy as it sounds.* For some people, information is enough. They're ready to take the ball and run with it. But for others, more is involved.

Some of you have found the information in this book to be confirming. It describes what you're already doing, and you feel encouraged to continue growing your marriage God's way. Others have found direction from these pages. You see areas that need attention, and you will begin to do some things differently. Change may be slow, but step-by-step, you're working together to gradually reclaim the marriage God has intended for you to have. Others are still stuck. You realize your marriage could be better and that change is needed. You even have the desire to change. But you just can't seem to do it. You feel powerless—and change seems out of reach.

If you're stuck, ask yourself why. What is it that prevents you from establishing a life for your marriage? Prioritizing, emotionally investing in your relationship, spending time together, listening and really hearing—why is it so difficult? If this is where you are, there's a reason. And when there's a reason, there's a solution. It may not be easy, and you may need help to both see the reason and find the solution. But God is faithful, and so are His people.

If you're stuck, get help. Let a professional help you explore issues and guide you toward solutions. The Lord always desires the best for His people. And He wants you to experience the marriage He has planned for you.

Conclusion

A Golden Opportunity

We hear a lot about mentors and models today. Mentors and models are beneficial to many professions, but they are especially valuable in the ministry. Every young minister needs someone to look up to who models a fruitful ministry. While there are some basics in the structure of ministry, there are also constant adjustments due to the changing world we live in. Ministry is a work in progress. Wise is the minister who looks at what is being done effectively in the world and then gleans ideas that enhance his ministry.

Most of us learn best from someone who is being successful at what we are trying to do. If you and I are successfully mixing ministry and marriage, it will bring us great pleasure and be an encouragement and model for those who are watching us.

Many of those who sit in the pews have never seen a functional family. This makes your glass house a golden opportunity for your congregants to peer inside and see how a healthy family relates.

Please Look In

When the world peers in through the glass walls of your parsonage, let it see the difference God's grace makes. Most folks would rather see a sermon any day than hear one. Let them look. Let them see 1 Cor. 13:4-7 lived out in your home:

> Love is patient, love is kind. It does not envy, it does not boast, it is not proud. It is not rude, it is not self-seeking, it is not easily angered, it keeps no record of wrongs. Love does not delight in evil but rejoices with the truth. It always protects, always trusts, always hopes, always perseveres.

Are you a loving husband who comes home and treats your wife kindly even when you're physically weary and mentally frustrated? Are you giving your children your time and attention?

Are you a wife and mother who musters up a warm greeting to your husband after a long, demanding day? Is your glass house a model of God's grace?

When those around you see you treating each other with patience and kindness, it will get their attention. Instead of rudeness, let them see courtesy and kindness. They'll note the absence of anger. They'll sense the security that your protective love for one another provides. And they'll want to know how they can get to that place. Let the world see God's grace in your life, your ministry, and your marriage.